my daughter
Rehtaeh Parsons

my daughter
Rehtaeh Parsons

Glen Canning
with Susan McClelland

GOOSE LANE EDITIONS

Edited by Matthew Halliday.
Cover and page design by Julie Scriver.
Cover photograph of Rehtaeh Parsons by Glen Canning.
Printed in Canada by Marquis.
10 9 8 7 6 5 4 3 2 1

Library and Archives Canada Cataloguing in Publication

Title: My daughter Rehtaeh Parsons / Glen Canning with Susan McClelland.
Names: Canning, Glen, 1963- author. | McClelland, Susan, author.
Identifiers: Canadiana (print) 20210107723 | Canadiana (ebook) 20210111909 |
ISBN 9781773101484 (softcover) | ISBN 9781773101491 (EPUB)
Subjects: LCSH: Parsons, Rehtaeh, 1995-2013. | LCSH: Parsons, Rehtaeh, 1995-2013—Mental health. | LCSH: Victims of bullying—Nova Scotia—Halifax—Biography. | LCSH: Cyberbullying. | LCSH: Bullying. | LCSH: Bullying—Prevention. | LCSH: Sexual consent. | LCSH: Teenage girls— Mental health. | LCSH: Teenage girls—Suicidal behavior. | LCGFT: Biographies.
Classification: LCC HV6773.15.C92 C36 2021 | DDC 302.34/3092—dc23

Goose Lane Editions acknowledges the generous support of the Government of Canada, the Canada Council for the Arts, and the Government of New Brunswick.

Goose Lane Editions
500 Beaverbrook Court, Suite 330
Fredericton, New Brunswick
CANADA E3B 5X4
gooselane.com

MIX
Paper from
responsible sources
FSC® C103567

This book is dedicated with love
to the memory of Rehtaeh Anne Parsons
and to every person struggling alone in a dark place.

Rage against that darkness and
know that you are not raging alone.

The names and any identifying characteristics of the youth in this book, except for immediate family, have been changed. The writers took some liberties in terms of recreating conversations. The section on Rehtaeh's stay at the IWK mental health facility 4 South uses actual quotes taken from her medical file.

Introduction

When a child dies, a parent breaks. A part of us has been torn away; life ceases to make sense, if it ever did. We see our children in ghostly shadows, hear their voices in quiet moments, and live with a constant pain — a pain we may even believe we deserve, having let them go. Most of all we simply ask why.

When my daughter, Rehtaeh Parsons, whom we all called Rae, died by suicide on April 7, 2013, I had at least a partial answer to that question. Seventeen months earlier, at the age of fifteen, she had attended a small party with four boys around her age. They were boys she thought she could trust, who went to her school, and who knew her friends, including the girl who introduced her to them. Rehtaeh left that house the following day believing she had been sexually assaulted, after a confusing and nightmarish night.

Rae's death was accompanied by a media frenzy uncharacteristic of the small Nova Scotia suburb where she lived. That was thanks in large part to a Facebook post Rae's mother, Leah, posted when our daughter was dying in the hospital, which brought first local, and soon national and global, attention to our family. There was also, of course, the famous photograph, taken on the night of her encounter with those boys: it depicts Rae hanging out the window after having thrown up, with a boy up against her, grinning and giving a thumbs-up to the camera. Both were naked from the waist down.

It had been broadcast across social media and beyond, but rather than a source of shame for the boys, it became one for her. Circulated until her death, it resulted in endless bullying and threats to her physical safety, particularly from other girls. It was not only the events of that night that led Rae to her death, but the ostracism that followed and the compounding failures of our criminal justice, mental health, and school systems to support her as she needed. Rae struggled to comprehend the culture of online harassment that followed her from school to school. Eventually she came to feel she could never outrun it.

This book is not about sexual assault, exactly, though it is in part: Canada's Department of Justice reports that thirty-seven women and girls out of every thousand have experienced sexual violence, the majority being young women between fifteen and twenty-five. In all likelihood, these numbers dramatically under-represent the problem, since the majority of assault survivors never report the crimes, for fear of being disbelieved, shunned, or shamed.

Nor is this book entirely about the institutional failures that let Rae down — though we are supposed to live in a country where these systems protect the weakest, not abandon them.

It is, more than anything else, about a culture that has normalized and accepted gender violence; a culture in which even women and girls play a role in perpetuating and normalizing that violence. After Rae's death, I plummeted too, into my own darkness. This book is partly about my awakening to understand how I too lived much of my life under the sway of a toxic, dysfunctional masculinity. It is about how men and women and boys and girls suffer due to it, and a patriarchal society that enables it.

I, like all of us, was born into this culture. Growing up, I was always an outlier, but never aware why. I tried so hard, growing up in a military family and then as a naval diver myself, to conform to the kinds of damaging cultural norms that so hurt Rae, and which continue to endanger other young people. Rae's death forced me to look deeper within at my own family and my own self.

This book is about Rae, but it's also about how all of us, hopefully, may begin putting ourselves back together.

Prologue
August 2011

In the summer of 2011, I took Rae and my wife, Krista, to Cozumel, an island off Mexico's eastern coast. Ten days in an all-inclusive hotel, nestled beside the jungle, just a cobblestone pathway from the beach and the Caribbean Sea. Around us was life: broad-leafed trees, lizards the size of dogs, hobbling turtles, birds painted like rainbows, and meandering garden beds blanketed in blood reds, brilliant magentas, lapis lazuli blues, and sun yellows. There was even an alligator that lived in our hotel's pond. The three of us spent the days serenaded by soprano crickets, baritone frogs, and symphonies of birdsong.

Since I could remember, I had been haunted by something buried within me, something I sensed but couldn't see. It was as if I had been living half a life, part of me closed to myself. But not on this trip. On this trip I was whole.

While we were there, I taught Rae one of my life's passions: scuba diving.

I always told people there was a silence that grew the further one descended in the oceans. The sounds of the earthly world — the roar of cars, the buzz of electrical wires, the static and voices of the surface world — were replaced with a soft hum. I once told Rae I believed that hum was in the key of C major; the key, I told her, that spiritualists believed was the sound of the universe moving.

I had to buy Rae a special oversized scuba mask, like the bug-faced ones underwater explorer Jacques Cousteau wore in the 1950s, because her glasses wouldn't fit under the newer models. Above water, the scuba instructor and I teased Rae that she'd scare the fish away, looking like a character in *Twenty Thousand Leagues Under the Sea.* But down there, the fish didn't care what she looked like, and a world of sea turtles and seahorses and fish of all sorts and sizes and colours unfolded for her.

Rae reminded me on this trip that she wanted to be a marine biologist. She had done a presentation in grade 8 on the overfishing of sharks, and even met with a professor at a local university who was an expert on them. In Cozumel, over a buffet of fried and grilled fish and plump, fresh fruits one night, Rae recounted some of what she'd been reading about the collapse of ocean ecosystems: "The oceans are a mess, Dad. We've killed them. Without the seas we won't survive, so I guess..." She drifted off. I thought for a moment she was going to cry. "I guess we killed ourselves," she finally said.

I nodded. Rae wasn't wrong, and whenever I discovered that she knew more about some aspects of the world than I did, I was proud of her, and a bit sad. I knew the day was nearing when she would no longer need me.

Animals had always been Rae's singular passion, but on most topics she was thoughtful, intellectually precocious, and relentlessly curious. (She was, of course, also a giggly teenager, about to start high school, boy-crazy and chatty.) I was proud of her and always had been. Her mother, Leah, and I had vowed to do all we could to raise her to feel safe, to explore within herself and in the wider world, to take risks and live her fullest life. She was a voracious reader, a builder of backyard mazes, a thinker and a questioner, interested in science, physics, the universe, God, and how it all might fit together.

She got this at least in part from her grandfather on Leah's side. An Anglican reverend, Ron Parsons was a man whose gentle, thoughtful curiosity made him almost the opposite of my own father. Rae was not quite ten years old when Reverend Ron died in 2005, at age seventy-eight. Her interest in science and worlds beyond our own came from school, from her reading, even from my own love of science fiction. But that early questioning of spirituality came from Reverend Ron. He would reference Psalm 139. "I have many anxious thoughts but God knows them all. I need to hand them over, let go and allow him to guide me." He added his own thoughts: "Then you will see the beauty inside and outside yourself. Then the soul awakens and becomes."

During those ten days in Cozumel, I managed to surrender my dark thoughts and just live in the moment. At night, Rae and I lay on lawn chairs and stared up at the Milky Way, its dusty skirt stretching from one end of the horizon to the other. On one side of us were somersaulting ocean waves, and on the other, the night calls of the forest.

"Dad," Rae said on our final evening, "do you believe in parallel universes?"

I laughed. Rae had been reading Stephen Hawking's *A Brief History of Time*. For a while, all she talked about was dark matter, black holes, and quantum mechanics.

"I don't know enough," I replied.

"Dad," my then fifteen-year-old said with a sigh. She explained that parallel universes may exist alongside our own, unobserved. Space and time may be radically different in them, operating with different physical properties or laws of physics. There may even, she said, be other versions of us in some of them. "You know that feeling of déjà vu?" she asked. "Maybe that's you, having experienced something in another universe."

Eventually she fell silent. Moments passed, and she spoke again: "I'm glad we're in this universe, Dad. I'm glad I chose you."

In the days and months that followed, this conversation would come back to haunt me, like she knew she was going somewhere else. But in the moment, I was simply glad that I had chosen her too.

Chapter One

The morning of November 14, 2011, I was waiting on the tarmac at the Halifax airport, readying for takeoff. Hours later, I would arrive in Ottawa, where I would spend a few days with my mother and siblings. Besides me and my older brother, Steve, my entire family lived in and around the nation's capital. There was Jim, who, after a prosperous career in computing, had retired young with his wife, Shari, and kids, Julia and Tyler, to a sprawling home on what Rae called "millionaires' row," a neighbourhood in suburban Kanata that was home to NHL stars and other Canadian celebrities. There was my sister, Kim, who lived nearby with her husband, Claudio, and daughter, Nikki. Mom lived down the road in Stittsville. And Casey, the youngest, lived not far away, on the city's outskirts. But emotionally, it felt as if he lived on the other side of the planet. He spent less time with the family than anyone, drank too much, and was frequently angry, bitter, and brooding.

A few days wasn't long, but Rae and I had rarely spent that long apart. The longest that we were ever out of touch was a month, when I had to travel from Corpus Christi, Texas, to Europe. For twenty-five years, I was in the Canadian Armed Forces. For twenty of those years, I was a mine clearance diver. My job was to clear sea mines — sweeping the bottom of the North Sea for mines set by the Nazis during World War II, for instance. That's exactly what I was doing in 1998 when Rae and I were apart that time. I had been afraid that when I did finally speak to her again, Rae, only two, wouldn't remember me. When my ship finally disembarked in Plymouth, England, I ran straight to one of those classically English red telephone boxes and slipped every coin I had into the machine.

"Dah," Rae said, coming on the phone. "Where you?" I breathed a sigh of relief. She remembered.

When I arrived back at my home base in Shearwater, Nova Scotia, Leah brought a tiny Rae to me, yawning and stretching after having been asleep in her car seat. Once out of the car, on shaky, tired legs, Rae moved toward me. A few feet in front of me, she stopped. Her back stiffened and her eyes darted from the ground and back to Leah as she dug a hole in the sand with the toe of her running shoe. Dread washed over me. She *had* forgotten. I moved and kneeled down in front of her. "I'm your dad," I said. "Dah. Do you remember me?"

She giggled, flicked her hand loose from Leah's and leapt into my arms, squeezing my neck so hard she left red marks on my skin.

In the late winter of 1995, Leah and I realized we were better off as friends than partners. We had only been together a few months, and what we didn't know when we went our separate ways was that she was pregnant. Leah and I were both thrilled when we discovered we were having a baby. We both wanted Rae, and we believed we were meant to come together, not romantically, but for a child.

Leah raised Rae in Reverend Ron's house in Cole Harbour, a 1960s ranch-style bungalow with a weeping evergreen set in a wide front yard. Cole Harbour was founded in 1754, a few years after the city of Halifax. Once a small village, Cole Harbour had ballooned into a suburb within Halifax's bigger metropolitan region, and like other communities on the east side of Halifax Harbour, the area was mostly middle class, a mix of blue- and white-collar. The nearby Shearwater naval base was a major source of employment, and plenty of Rae's classmates had parents who worked for the military. I retired from the navy myself on July 1, 2009, at the age of forty-six. A few years before that, knowing I would be young enough for a second career, I had returned to another love of mine: photography. I worked part-time for the *Daily News* in Halifax. I was set to go full-time when the newspaper folded. I went back to college to become a videographer, and for about a year I was a cameraman for CTV News in Halifax. I wasn't part of the union, so I was mostly working night shifts and weekends, leaving me little time for Rae or my wife, Krista. In 2012, I began working at the Apple Store in the Halifax Shopping Centre, which gave me a small salary and enough freedom with my work schedule to take short trips, like this one to Ottawa.

Cole Harbour was an idyllic place to grow up, but Leah and I worried about its cultural uniformity — it was a safe enclave where mostly white, middle-class families raised their kids in a more or less homogenous environment. It was important, both for Leah and for me, to make sure Rae felt free to explore, to question, to become her own self. Above all else, I never wanted her to feel about her home as I'd felt about mine growing up.

Throughout our childhoods, all four of my siblings plotted their escapes from the family home, as did I. Our father, Thornton Canning, was a model of 1960s masculinity: unapproachable and disciplinarian, as unrelenting as the rocky coast of Nova Scotia. He showed no wobbles, fears, or insecurities. He was born in Parrsboro, Nova Scotia, in 1939, and at that time, Parrsboro was a sleepy town where men fished or worked in the mill. Parrsboro was predominantly inhabited by descendants of British, Irish, and some French settlers. My dad's ancestors were among the first settler families in the area, coming from Cork, Ireland, in 1753. When they arrived, the area's Indigenous people, the Mi'kmaq, were still fighting the British to hold on to their lands across the region. My family surname wasn't Canning back then, but Cannon — family folklore posits that our name was changed because one of our early ancestors wanted to avoid repaying a debt. Rae, from the moment she was born, looked Irish, with those big blue eyes, high chiseled cheekbones, and dark hair.

My dad was the youngest of five siblings, and he spent most of his childhood running in the fields and attending school intermittently. In that time and place, school wasn't a top priority for rural kids, who were needed on the farm, and who would usually go on to work the same jobs as their fathers and grandfathers. My father helped his own dad in the mill. Generations of Parrsboro men also worked in shipbuilding, or in the coal mines. But by the 1950s, all of these industries were on the wane: steel ships replaced wooden ones, gas replaced coal. With his limited education, my dad had few choices when he turned eighteen. He joined the Royal Canadian Air Force, completing basic training in Cold Lake, Alberta.

He met my mother, Ivy Elliot, when he was on leave from a course he was taking at Canadian Forces Base Borden in Ontario. It was a smouldering summer day, on a side road near Wasaga Beach, north of Toronto. As Dad's car passed, one of Mom's friends shouted out, "Hey dreamboat!" But when my dad's friend stopped the car, the same friend giggled and said, "Not you, shipwreck. The one in the passenger seat." The woman was referring to my dad, not the driver. My mom and dad wrote letters to each other for a year before they reconnected in person. They went on five dates and decided to marry.

I was born at a military hospital in Baden-Baden, Germany, in 1963. My dad was stationed there at Four Wing Air Force Base as an air technician, fixing fighter jets. Not long after I was born, my dad was transferred back to Cold Lake. He wasn't earning enough money to support his growing family: my older brother, Steve; followed by me; then Jim; then Kim; and finally, Casey. For a while, Dad held down three jobs: technician by day, pizza delivery man by night, and guitar teacher by night and weekend. He knew he couldn't keep up that pace — he was tired and thus foggy-eyed on the job that mattered most — so he applied to go back to school to become an officer, giving him a bigger paycheque. He earned a bachelor of engineering degree, specializing in aerospace, at the University of Alberta, and followed it up with a master's degree in aerospace engineering from the University of California, Los Angeles. Afterwards we moved to Trenton, Ontario, where he held his first post as an officer in the air force. Then, in my final year of high school, we moved to St. Louis, Missouri, where he was one of the aerospace engineers tasked with overseeing the Canadian government's purchase of the CF-18 fighter jets.

My father's life was about his work, and as a military man, that meant keeping order. He felt it was his responsibility to tell his four sons, and my little sister, Kimmy, what we were to do in life, and for his sons, that meant traditional, masculine paths. When I announced as a child that I wanted to be a photographer rather than join the army, he just stared at me until I acquiesced. My brother Jim was, on the surface, a son he could be prouder of: the star running back on the high-school football team, good-looking, and a magnet for girls. But he had to hide from my father that he often preferred to spend nights alone in his room, designing flowcharts for computer programming.

At eighteen, I escaped the family home, but not my father's planned path for me. At my eighteenth birthday dinner in St. Louis, I had a plane ticket tucked in my shirt pocket, and a copy of the oath I would have to swear to join the Canadian Armed Forces. But I found my own way within that world — a year after my basic training, I switched into the navy because I preferred diving to combat. A few years earlier, I'd joined the Flying Frogmen Scuba Club in Trenton, one of the oldest diving clubs in the country, and for several summers, all I did was dive, first in swimming pools and then in nearby lakes, looking for treasures in the sunken steamships which, before highways and railways, brought goods to Northern Ontario. All I ever found was broken glass, pottery, and a few old Coke bottles.

Even after my siblings and I were gone, my mother remained in my father's shadow, subservient and submissive — if you reached the answering machine, you would hear her voice saying, "You've reached

Tony Canning." After my father died in 2006, my mother seemed reborn, making new friends and taking up new hobbies. *Unstoppable* was the word she once used to describe her new life.

On the plane, I began to doze off, thinking of my mother, when a flight attendant tapped my arm: "Sir, you need to shut off your phone." When I looked down, I saw that Rae had texted:

> Dad, you know how you said I could come and live with you and Krista anytime. Now. Can I come now?

I groaned.

Rae and I had talked about her living with Krista and me, but she wasn't allowed to move in simply because she and Leah had fought. Leah and I had come to an agreement early in Rae's life not to be the kind of separated parents who used their child as a proxy in a battle between them. If Leah and Rae were fighting over her messy room or her curfew — which they were doing a lot since Rae graduated junior high — they'd have to sort it out. I wrote back quickly.

> What's wrong?

Rae's response came fast and riddled with typos, like she was typing frantically.

> Don ask me question if you love me and your my father, you have to do this for me.

> > Tell me what's wrong?

> Dad please. You promised. Let me live with you.

> > I'm on the plane. I have to turn my phone off.
> > Tell me what is going on?

> You have to let me come and live with you and Krista. You're supposed to be my father. You are supposed to help.

The attendant returned, bent down, and asked more firmly, "Sir, can you turn off your phone? We're about to take off."

> Rae, I will call you when I get to Ottawa.
> I won't have wifi for an hour.

> If you love me you will just do it. Please. Just do it. Now. Say
> I can live with you.

I called Rae when the plane landed, but there was no answer. I tried again between periods at the Ottawa Senators game that night — Jim had scored some front-row tickets. For the next two days, Rae ignored my texts and voicemails, but I was almost too busy to notice, seeing the family I saw so little, bringing my mother to a doctor's appointment and running errands for her.

On my last night, our after-dinner conversation turned to Casey: his anger, his aggression, his drinking. None of us understood his alcoholism for what it was: a symptom of something terrible and unspoken. He had become convinced that something awful had happened to him, or to all of us, when we were children. He'd claimed that a relative of ours molested him; none of us believed it. Casey drank, he said, to still his anxiety and spiralling thoughts, which none of us really understood. A few years earlier, when I had taken Krista to meet my family, a similar evening had taken place. My family and I took turns lambasting Casey's reliance on drink, his dysfunction. Finally Jim turned to Krista and asked her what she thought. Krista, one of those rare people who doesn't really speak unless she has something to say, thought for a moment and said, "I think there's a lot of judgment in the room."

It was like we had all been slapped. She and I had only been together a little while, and it was brave of her to say something like that. But she was right. We didn't want to dwell on his pain and his anger, so we did the next worst thing: we ignored him and his accusations. On the flight back to Nova Scotia, all I thought about was my quickness to judgment — about how I avoided things I didn't understand.

I tried Rae again that Friday evening, November 18, sitting in my Fiat in the airport parking lot after arriving back in Halifax.

Still no answer.

Like any teenager, as Rae grew older she began challenging Leah and me — especially Leah. She was rebelling against Leah's house rules, being messier than she would normally, sneaking out at night to watch YouTube videos with neighbourhood friends. Rae was finding herself and defining herself, not as a daughter but as a young adult.

When Rae was little, she described me to Leah as a comfy, well-worn, oversized sweatshirt that kept her warm. And to me, Rae described Leah as a protecting angel. But I knew there would come a time when I wouldn't be Rae's comforter anymore, and Rae wouldn't want Leah guiding her every move. So I figured Rae wasn't replying to my voice and text messages because she just didn't want to. She had a wide circle of friends, many of whom she'd known since kindergarten, as well as budding friendships with teens she was just meeting in high school.

That was it, I convinced myself.

Still, I couldn't wait any longer to hear her voice. I called Leah's landline, hoping to find out where Rae was and why she was ignoring me. The phone rang and rang. I was about to hang up when Marianne, Leah's sister, picked up. A sociology professor at Saint Mary's University in Halifax, Marianne usually spoke with force and confidence, like every conversation was a lecture. Tonight, though, her voice was thin and scratchy, and, for a moment, I didn't recognize her. I thought I had dialed the wrong number. "Oh Glen," she stammered. "Where...where are you?"

The desperation in her voice sent a wave of panic through me. "What's wrong?" I demanded.

"It's the worst, Glen. The absolute worst."

I fell quiet and listened to Marianne sob. "What is it?" I eventually asked in a soft voice, thinking something had happened to Leah.

"It's Rae."

I choked, coughed, and gripped the steering wheel hard. "What's wrong with Rae?" I asked through gritted teeth.

"It just happened. I mean...we just found out. Rae and Leah need to tell you. It can't come from me. Can, can you come here, now?" My mind ran through all the possibilities: Rae was sick. She had been diagnosed with cancer. Did she even have a doctor's appointment this week? There has been an accident. A car hit her.

"I'm...I'm coming," I sputtered. I slammed down the phone and started the car.

I had never felt anything but joy in Leah's home, but as I pulled up and saw Leah's white minivan parked in the street, a foreboding overwhelmed me.

As I walked up the steps and saw Rae's old tire swing swaying in the breeze, I caught an image of her as a small child: long, wiry legs stretched through the tube, one flip-flop on, the other kicked off into the grass, her long hair sweeping the ground as she leaned back and spun around.

Leah opened the door as soon as I knocked.

"Rae's at Marianne's," Leah began hurriedly. "We thought Rae needed to be somewhere quieter." The rescue dogs Leah was caring for were barking from some back room. Leah was speaking fast and her back was flush up against the wall, like it was holding her up. "We have an appointment with the RCMP on Saturday."

I blinked. "What?" I couldn't put Leah's words together. "What are you saying?"

She told me, and my eyes didn't move from Leah's face. Her usually smooth skin looked flushed and mottled. The whites in her eyes were runny red, her brown irises dull and distant.

"There's more. There's a photo going around of it. Of Rae. Kids are sharing it with each other. She's not wearing all her clothes and a boy..." Leah stopped.

"A boy what?" I shouted.

"A boy is doing stuff to her," Leah said.

I suddenly realized I was sweating. I took off my jacket and let it fall to the ground.

Leah managed to explain that, because of a photo taken during the incident, Rae was receiving texts and social-media messages from teens at her school saying she was a slut and a whore. Boys were asking her for a repeat performance, and girls were writing that if they ever saw her again, they would beat her up.

"I knew something was wrong, something was off, all week, but Rae only just told me. I thought she was sick." Leah stuffed a fist into her mouth to stifle her cries. "She's at Marianne's. We hoped, we thought, the quiet might be good for her."

"When... when did it happen?" I was trying to comprehend all of this, to connect the dots. Where was Rae that this could have happened? I couldn't think.

"It happened last weekend at Amanda's sleepover," Leah said, as if reading my thoughts.

I swallowed hard. Now I remembered. The sleepover was why Rae and I didn't see each other before I left for Ottawa. Rae had been excited for the sleepover with her new friend, Amanda, whom she had met in September when she started at Cole Harbour District High School. I hadn't wanted to dampen Rae's spirits by holding her to our commitment to spend the night together. Rae had said Amanda "sparkled," the way some girls do. She was strawberry blonde and socially connected. Rae had used the word *popular*. Amanda dated, boys liked to talk to her, she wore makeup and went to parties. "She has experience," Rae told me.

"There is something else," Leah's words dug into me. "It wasn't just one boy." I blinked and nodded, as if to say *go on.*

"It might have been as many as four. Four boys might have raped our daughter."

I needed air. I couldn't breathe. "Can I...can I see Rae?" I eventually stammered.

In my mind's eye, I saw Rae when she was tiny, when I would tuck her in at night, wrapping around her the blue-and-white checkered quilt that my mom had made for me when I was a boy. Then I'd lie down beside her and read *Guess How Much I Love You,* or some other kid's book.

Tears pooled in both our eyes as Leah fumbled with her phone, her fingers shaking so much she had to dial Marianne's number twice. "Can Glen come?" she eventually croaked into the receiver. Leah looked up at me and nodded.

Walking into Marianne's house felt like falling. I was dizzy, my head swaying. My eyes blurred and then refocused as Rae came into view.

She was sitting at the end of Marianne's couch, her body slouched and small, her head down, her long hair, unbrushed and tangled, falling into her face. She was barefoot, wearing faded jeans and one of my old grey navy sweatshirts. She didn't look up. She didn't move. She didn't seem real, more like a wax figure.

"Hi Dad," she mumbled. She finally moved, to pull even tighter into herself.

"Can I sit down beside you?" I asked, my voice wavering.

"Uh-huh."

"Can I hug you?"

Her body shuddered but she whispered *yes.*

Rae's embrace was limp. She pulled away as soon as I loosened my hold.

Seeing Rae in such a state, it was like she had descended to the bottom of the ocean. And I felt Rae's descent with every part of my being, because, as I would discover years later, I was drowning alongside her. Then something grew from inside me, something from deep down on that ocean floor. Something all-consuming. Who did this to you? What are their names? I needed to know.

I stifled the questions. Instead, I decided I never wanted to know the names of the boys that had done this to her. I turned to Marianne. Swallowing all my pain, my rage that I knew, if released, would consume not just me but everyone and everything around me, I managed to get out, "How did this happen?" At that point, that information was all I could handle.

Chapter Two

That Friday afternoon, according to Leah, Rae, curled up on the kitchen floor in a fetal position, had told Leah everything that had happened, or at least what she could remember. The Saturday before, November 12, 2011, as she prepared to leave for her sleepover with Amanda, she and Leah had talked briefly about a German shepherd that had arrived at the SPCA where Rae was volunteering — her job was caring for the cats and walking the dogs. The German shepherd was about six months old, not fully grown, and had the largest feet Leah, who ran a German shepherd rescue charity in addition to working as an animal enforcement officer, had ever seen on a dog, like diving flippers. They both laughed. By summer, they said, the puppy would be bigger than they were.

Then Leah asked what the girls would be doing on their sleepover. The usual, Rae said: taking selfies, posting messages on Instagram, messaging friends, doing their nails and makeup, watching movies. Leah asked if Rae had told Amanda that she didn't eat red meat. Amanda, Leah was informed, was ordering a vegetarian pizza.

Not long after five o'clock, Rae took a bus from Cole Harbour to nearby Eastern Passage, where Amanda lived. Like Leah's neighbourhood, Amanda's was quiet, full of sprawling boulevards lined with modest suburban houses. Kids played ball hockey all year long on these streets, channelling the Pittsburgh Penguins' Sidney Crosby, maybe the most famous person ever to come out of Cole Harbour.

It's easy to imagine a crowd of them out in the street, whooping and yelling, as Rae walked from the bus stop to Amanda's house. The last of the season's raked leaves would have been pushed into brown paper bags and set by the curbs, to be picked up by the city.

Rae and Amanda didn't know each other before high school, but Amanda knew one of Rae's closest elementary-school friends from soccer. In middle school, Rae's friends were all good students. But, according to Rae, they lacked whatever it was that the popular girls in school had; whatever it was that made boys take notice, talk to them, take them seriously. Rae's squad was too boring for the wild kids and too mainstream for the outliers. That fall, Rae and her friends from junior high and elementary school had spread out. They were still friends, or so Rae thought, but they were exploring new relationships, new worlds, that were taking them in different directions.

Before the start of high school, Rae had written in her journal about how excited she was. She wanted a more typical high-school experience than her friends did: Friday-night football games, house parties, prom, joining the cheer team. She even made a time capsule of her goals for high school. Above all else: she wanted to have a boyfriend. Amanda was a step toward that new life. Cole Harbour High had overwhelmed Rae at first. She had gone from a middle school of two hundred kids, where everyone knew each other, to a high school that merged the graduates of several middle schools, from several neighbourhoods, into one. Her grade alone numbered more than 350 students. But when Rae found Amanda, she liked her immediately. Amanda dressed like Rae's lifelong friends, in plain T-shirts, faded black jeans, plain hoodies, and Converse sneakers. But she had, said Rae, "star power."

At some point during the sleepover, Amanda suggested they go for a walk. They hadn't gone far when Amanda stopped. She told Rae she wanted to visit some friends, gesturing to a house nearby.

Brothers lived there, Amanda said, Zachery and Dylan. She had dated one of them, though she didn't like him anymore. "He's a dick," she told Rae. He had flirted with other girls, texting them, and she wanted to make him regret it.

The door to the house swung open before the girls reached it. A light came on, and a guy leapt out wearing a tight, plain white T-shirt that showed off his teenaged muscles. His hair was dirty blonde and looked windswept. He waved for Amanda and Rae to come in. "That's Brandon," Amanda whispered to Rae. Brandon, Amanda explained, was a friend of one of the brothers who lived there. The way Amanda said Brandon's name, it sounded to Rae as if she had dated him, too.

The inside of the house smelled of boys: cheap cologne and dirty socks. Brandon waved his arm toward another guy as the girls moved into the kitchen. This new boy was a smaller version of Brandon. He had darker hair, and was shovelling french fries from a Styrofoam container into his mouth.

Amanda was going on at length about how annoying their science teacher was. He was a bully and picked favourites, she said. After that, she moved on to trash-talking a girl who was a cheerleader, but at the bottom of the pyramid. Fat, the girl was fat, she thought she heard Amanda say, and kind of loose. While she was talking, Amanda slipped off her jacket and tossed it on the couch behind Brandon, who was swaying while he listened.

The other, smaller guy introduced himself as Zachery, and he passed Rae a glass filled with what he said was vodka. She stared into the clear liquid. Zachery did a shot and smiled, as if to demonstrate what Rae should do too. Amanda was still chatting as Brandon inched his way closer to Rae.

Rae looked down at the glass again, then at Amanda, who had finally stopped talking and was pouring herself her own drink, downing it all in one shot. Slowly, Rae drank as well.

As she continued to drink, she looked at those boys. They were very different than her friends Paul and Antoni, whom she'd just met that fall at Cole Harbour High. Paul and Antoni were smaller physically, and awkward around other kids, but nice around parents.

Antoni was a stoner, if she had to label him, and Paul a music nerd. Paul and Antoni liked talking science with Rae. Later, Rae told Leah that, looking back, she felt that girls didn't fit into Brandon and Zachery's world as "friends."

Most of that evening was a blackout for Rae, who had little experience with alcohol. She knew she woke up the next morning on a bed, in a basement bedroom, between two boys she didn't know and didn't remember meeting the night before. Her clothes were on backwards and her glasses — which she rarely took off, even to sleep — were on a night table, suggesting someone else had placed them there. She fixed her clothes and fumbled her way to the door, her head pierced by pain from a hangover, her legs weak and shaking. She found her Uggs in a mess of other shoes, all large boys' running shoes. She stumbled in a daze to a bus stop, and when she was back at Leah's house she crept back into bed, unsure of what had happened the night before, if anything. She did remember kissing someone and someone else on top of her. She also recalled throwing up at some point, out a window, as she hit her head on the frame. It still hurt.

Her only communication that day was with her friend Beth. "I fucked up," she texted her. Because Rae remembered so little, she told me later, she felt at first that she had done something wrong.

Rae told Leah, then later on me, and eventually the police, that she didn't know what exactly had happened. She was there, and then gone. She didn't know where Amanda went. Had she even tried to help? Had she abandoned her there, in that house? Did she know Rae was in trouble? Was Amanda in trouble too?

It was like the lights turned off and then on again, she would later tell me. "It was like the time when you did a training exercise for the navy," she reminded me. "When you had to use the broken equipment that made you breathe in bad air." She was talking about a rebreathing naval exercise that involved me briefly losing consciousness. I had told Rae that unlike sleep, during which a person retains a sense of the passage of time, when I woke during the exercise I didn't know if I'd been unconscious for seconds, minutes, hours, or days. "It felt the same for me," she said. "I was drinking and then gone, until I woke up between those boys."

Chapter Three

Leah took Rae to the RCMP's Cole Harbour detachment that weekend for an interview with police. Constable Kim Murphy ushered them into an interview room and wrote down the facts as Rae told them to her. Constable Murphy, Rae said, had a kind face and soft eyes.

In that interview, Rae talked mostly about the picture that had circulated during the past week: her throwing up, leaning semi naked out a window, with Brandon thrust up against her back. Rae had learned that the boys were sending the picture around and boasting about how they got lucky. But it was the girls, including friends Rae had believed she could trust, who were relentless in their attacks over text and social media, calling her a slut. Rae was focused on wanting the picture confiscated and the cyberharassment to stop so she could return to school.

Leah and Rae left that first interview feeling buoyant. The police were taking the case seriously, they thought.

Then, on November 22, another police officer, Detective Constable Patricia Snair of the Halifax Regional Police, called Leah. Officer Snair said that her unit, the Sexual Assault Investigation Team, had been handed the file. (Halifax is one of only a few cities in Canada in which municipal policing is an integrated system, with both the federal RCMP and a municipal force — Rae's case was investigated by a combined team, including members of both forces.)

"Did they stop the picture from being sent around?" Rae asked, when Leah got off the phone.

Leah shook her head.

Rae folded her arms across her chest, tilted her head, and looked at her mother quizzically.

"I guess that RCMP detective, Murphy, shouldn't have conducted a formal interview," Leah began. "You have to do the interview again." Rae's shoulders slackened. She cursed and then she started shaking her head and murmuring *no*.

This was the first of many mistakes that would dog the investigation. In 2015, former Ontario assistant attorney general Murray Segal produced an independent review of Rae's case for the Nova Scotia government. In it, he excoriated the police handling of the case, right from the first interview. Segal wrote: "Rehtaeh provided a lengthy, non-recorded statement to the responding police officer before the case was assigned to a specialized investigator from the sexual assault unit. This did not follow proper protocol. Because Rehtaeh was a young person, she should have been interviewed only once, alongside a social worker from the Department of Community Services. Instead, the officer who first responded to the complaint unnecessarily interviewed her at length, and did so in the presence of Rehtaeh's mother, who should have been interviewed separately."

Segal also noted that, because it was un-recorded, there was no way to know how the interview was conducted — did the officer use leading questions to direct Rae's answers? And were the notes reflective of Rae's answers, or merely Constable Murphy's interpretation of them?

When Rae learned she'd have to do another interview, she dropped to the kitchen floor, tucked her knees up into her chest, and started rocking back and forth. "I can't do this," she murmured. "Is it because they don't believe me?" Leah got down on her own knees and rubbed Rae's back.

After the first interview with Murphy, Rae had turned off her phone. She wanted to staunch the flow of messages from her classmates. But that night, on an impulse, she turned the phone back on. Three days' worth of text messages and Instagram and Facebook messages. She stared at her screen as they filed in, pinging and buzzing one after the other, like dominoes falling. Some of the senders were anonymous, but it was clear that most were from students at Cole Harbour High, friends and peers, and the attacks were escalating.

You had a foursome with my friends. What about me?

You slut. You tried to steal our boyfriends. We're going to come after you.

We have the photo and we're making sure everyone gets it

At first, Rae tried to respond:

You have the wrong girl. What happened wasn't my fault. I was taken advantage of. It wasn't my fault.

But soon the volume of messages dwarfed her attempts to reply. And the messages weren't just from strangers. A friend of Amanda's wrote:

You did this to hurt Amanda. You were jealous of her life, her community. You are just such trash. We will follow you with this wherever you go. You will never have a life again.

And a girl named Patti, Rae's best friend throughout elementary school and middle school, with whom she had spent countless hours and weekend sleepovers, wrote on Rae's Facebook wall:

Sluts are not welcome here

Rae shrivelled up on the couch, this time wrapping her leopard blanket around herself.

Leah and I tried to console her, but she was almost catatonic, murmuring over and over again, "This will follow me everywhere." Leah and I were both worried that Rae simply wouldn't be able to get through the second police interview, not in the state she was in.

The medical report had come back stating that there was anal tearing, and bruising in the hips and around her ankles and wrists, like Rae had been tied or held down tightly. Rae had reported the incident to the police just shy of a week afterwards and had showered repeatedly, so there was no foreign DNA remaining on her body. But the doctor still suggested the physical marks on her skin indicated a violent attack. "It's like my body isn't mine and I don't know how to connect with it," she had told me the day of the doctor's appointment. Rae wouldn't talk about the appointment, so I didn't press for information. Leah said it was hard. Rae didn't let go of Leah's hand the entire time.

Nonetheless, a different narrative had emerged around Rae and all of us: that she had been asking for it, and that whatever happened to her had been her fault.

Leah called Amanda, hoping to stop the tidal wave of hateful messages. She told Amanda that if anything happened to Rae, she would hold Amanda responsible. Leah's uncharacteristic directness probably shocked Amanda, who started to cry. Amanda, sobbing, said to Leah it wasn't rape. Rae "wasn't screaming," Leah said, "so it wasn't rape: I know. I've been raped before."

Leah was rendered speechless, wondering how many girls had been raped in this small, peaceful community.

Amanda assured Leah she would do whatever she could to stop people from sending the photo around, and quickly got off the phone, leaving Leah momentarily optimistic that the onslaught would soon stop. But later that day, Amanda's mother called Leah — not to console her or show her support, but to berate her for calling a fifteen-year-old girl without her parents' permission and threatening her.

The photograph stayed in circulation, and the vitriol kept pouring toward Rae. Leah and I even started to get messages from teenagers we didn't know, telling us that Rae was lying to us. She had gone to that house to have sex with those boys and couldn't handle the shaming that came afterward. She wasn't raped, other parents started messaging us; she was conniving and manipulative.

She loved what happened to her. That's the kind of girl she is.

You don't even know your daughter. She went off with one of them at a party earlier in the summer.

A woman wrote on Facebook, saying that she knew the boys.

I don't know how Rae could have kept her hands off of them.

Another simply said:

She got what was coming to her.

Lifelong friends of Leah's, with children Rae's age, refused to get involved. Some explicitly took the boys' side, or just said the police would deal with it. They didn't want to know anything more about it.

Even the boys, bragging about their conquest, reached out to Rae, threatening her and warning against legal action. They didn't do anything, they said, and Rae would be the one in trouble in the end.

In a Facebook message from Brandon in early December 2011, some of the information Rae had been searching for was given to her: Amanda had come back to get her that night. Amanda, who had told Leah it wasn't rape — that Rae hadn't been "screaming" — had in fact seen what was going on.

Hey, umm, are you taking us to court over what happened? Because we didn't do anything wrong (well I didn't because I didn't take the picture obvs) anyway everyone forget about what happened and its not a big deal but you bring us to court, I can't see you winning when we didn't do anything wrong but like even Amanda told me that she knows what happened because when she came to get you and we were getting you to leave you wouldn't leave but anyway message me back please. I will give you my number if u want and u can call me about what's going on. Thanks!

Chapter Four

Over the following weeks, Rae showered over and over, scrubbing her skin, washing her hair, cleaning her nails with a coarse brush, all the while letting the water fill the bathtub. She would then sit in the tub, soaking until the temperature was tepid and her arms and legs were covered in goosebumps. She'd watch as the water drained, then she'd shower again, with scalding water that left her skin pink and puffy.

Leah made Rae's comfort foods: homemade pizza pockets, roast chicken, strudels, and vegetarian pastas. Leah changed Rae's sheets and cleaned her room, folding the laundry and vacuuming — but left a bit of the mess so it still felt like Rae's home. Leah and I tried to get Rae back to a schedule of studying and homework; although she was too afraid to go to school, we encouraged her to move ahead at home in science and math, and maybe even study subjects she was interested in that they didn't teach in school, like oceanography and physics.

Teaghan, Rae's two-year old sister, moved around the house on her wobbly legs while Temyson, seven, practiced running the bases in preparation for winter softball training, skidding in her socks on the hardwood floors. Leah talked on the phone about finding homes for the rescue dogs, which yelped whenever someone came to the door. The dogs were mutts, both mid-sized adults with matted fur, one black and white, the other the colour of burnt wood.

Despite all this life around her, Rae said she never felt so far away.

I urged Rae to get out, see a movie with me, go for a bite, or a walk near Halifax Harbour to watch the ships come in. As a small child, she would build stories around where she thought those ships came from. Her stories were filled with the kind of antiquated tropes found in old pop culture: ships from India carrying warm spices and teas; from China, with hulls full of jade and silks in rich colours; and Russian ships full of nesting dolls. In all the stories she made up, one thing was the same: the ships contained runaway children, who each held a superpower unique to the country they were from. As a photojournalist for the *Daily News*, I was called on assignment one night to photograph a container that had come off a ship. Police reported it contained people who were trying to smuggle themselves into Canada. When I told Rae about those people, she broke down and cried. She said she could feel them, their desperation to risk their lives for freedom. She even wanted to meet them, to hear their stories. From an early age, she had great compassion and empathy for others.

I'd sit at the end of Rae's bed as she wrote in her diary or doodled sketches of sharks and dolphins. I'd leave when she fell asleep, her glasses always still on. But her sleep never lasted long and was punctuated by nightmares. Sometimes I stayed, to be there when she woke up, and when she did wake she would often be choking and perspiring, reaching for the hand of whoever was near her. When she stayed at my house with Krista and me, she would cry out in the night for me. I would come running and place my hand on her back. Just knowing Leah or I were nearby seemed to comfort her.

Rae took solace in her diary, flipping through the pages, re-reading her entries, sometimes out loud. It was like she was trying to reconnect with her past, trying to put herself back together again. Leah and I both knew Rae needed time to heal. She had to search for what brought her comfort. Leah and I talked about how we needed to remain steady, no matter what Rae might say.

I spent an afternoon with Rae in her room at Leah's house. Her shelves bulged with fantasy and sci-fi paperbacks, including a collection of Isaac Asimov novels that I'd given her, as well as science magazines and textbooks, and mementos like her stone and shell collections from camping trips in Nova Scotia and Mexico. On a chair she'd positioned her stuffed animals, including the hippopotamus Beanie Baby I had bought her when she visited me in Fort Walton Beach, Florida, where I was stationed. It was just after 9/11, and I was there on an explosives-training course with the US Navy. I talked to Rae about that trip, helping her revive childhood memories that inspired her dreams of becoming a vet or a marine biologist. She was six then, and I had taken her to a dolphin rehabilitation centre. Two of the dolphins, due to their age and injuries, couldn't be released. But they were gentle, and they were used for therapeutic programs for special-needs children, particularly those with autism. Rae and a staff member went swimming with a female dolphin named Daphne, who kissed Rae's cheek and danced in the water with her.

Rae was not neat, and the only place that was ever dusted in her room was the tiny table in the corner where she had placed the wooden box with the brass plate that bore the name of Jasper, her first dog, a cocker spaniel. Jasper's ashes were inside.

On the walls she'd pinned pictures of her life: ballet lessons (she was scowling in that photo, looking past the camera, probably at me, since she hated wearing tutus), gymnastics (she glowered in that photo too, probably because Leah and I were forcing her to do it after her initial enthusiasm had waned), and middle-school cheerleading (she'd been so proud to make the team and be accepted by the other members). There were pictures of Rae and Leah working at the SPCA. There were pictures of Rae and me the day she left the hospital as a newborn. There were pictures of Rae, Teaghan, and Temyson at a Halifax-area wildlife park. Finally, there were pictures of Rae's fifteenth birthday the previous December at Zen Cuisine, a Chinese restaurant: Rae's favourite. Both families were together, because for Rae we were always one. She ordered the lemon chicken, as always.

Rae and I dug out her scrapbook and together we watched her grow up all over again. We looked at pictures from her grade 9 graduation. In a short video she had filmed on my iPhone the afternoon of the ceremony, she talked further about her excitement for high school: studying science and math in advanced courses, taking a visual arts class to learn real painting techniques. Going to parties. Meeting new friends, and that boyfriend she wanted — he would be tall and dark-haired, like Taylor Lautner of the *Twilight* films.

Rae's second police interview was held on November 29, 2011. Unlike the first, at which Leah and Rae were together, Rae went in alongside a social worker.

In the initial interview with Constable Murphy, Rae was mostly concerned with stopping the photograph's circulation and the harassment she was facing. In her interview with Detective Constable Patricia Snair of the Halifax Regional Police, Rae focused on what she could remember from that night, including sitting up at some point and telling whoever was on top of her to stop. She also recalled vomiting.

Not long after the interview with Officer Snair, Rae and I were sitting in my living room. Krista was in the kitchen brewing a pot of coffee and fumbling with ingredients as she tried to make dinner. In the pauses in conversation, Krista would call out, "Pizza? Pasta? Sushi? Should we just order in?" Outside, snow was falling, soft and sticky. Since I had retired from the navy, I no longer had missions to warm places in the cold months — Spain, Southern France, Aruba — warm, sunny places to take Rae to break the monotony of the East Coast's wet and sloppy winters.

Rae asked me how the investigation would work. "Do you think the police are doing it right?" she asked.

My back stiffened. I knew what she was referring to. The day after their interview, Constable Murphy had called Leah to ask if Rae could get a copy of the photograph and send it to her. "I mean, Dad, isn't it the police officer's job to get the photograph and stop it?" she asked.

Inside I was thinking *absolutely*, but I didn't want to alarm Rae so I replied that Officer Murphy must know what she was doing.

Rae also talked to me about the message she had sent her friend Beth, saying she had "fucked up." She told me that referred to her regret at going to the boys' house in the first place. Officer Snair had probed Rae during the interview about that comment, however, questioning what she really meant. Beth, Rae also told me, had gone to a Cole Harbour High guidance counsellor, complaining about the photograph and saying Rae was being harassed in school. The guidance counsellor told Beth that because the incident happened off school grounds, and the photograph was being sent around virtually — i.e. not at school — it was out of the school's hands, and Beth shouldn't talk about it further.

It was early December, a week away from Rae's sixteenth birthday. The movie theatres were full of Academy Award contenders, and I suggested we skip dinner at home, grab something at the cinema, and hit up a double bill. I tempted Rae with double-buttered popcorn. Rae smiled and nodded, but then her shoulders caved in. "I don't remember much. I wish I remembered more because it's like my body remembers stuff that my head doesn't," she said.

"I know," I said with a sigh, reaching over and putting a hand on her shoulder. But in truth: I didn't know. I couldn't possibly imagine what she was going through. "You're seeing your counsellor soon?" I asked.

"Uh-huh." Rae had to be sixteen to be assigned a rape counsellor, partly due to limited resources, and also because those younger than sixteen needed more specialized child services. Leah had scheduled the appointment for the day of Rae's birthday on December 9.

Rae then asked me in a feeble voice if I thought the police weren't taking what happened to her seriously. I stared at her, stunned, in shock, that she would consider for a moment that the police would doubt her. "Are you kidding?" I finally cried out. Her face dropped. She wasn't. "Rae, why are you questioning this?" I asked, truly baffled.

I stared at Rae's slackening shoulders and was reminded of my years in the navy, of the culture that brewed among boys in groups and the code of silence among the higher-ups. On leave, many of the guys would head into nearby towns, pick bars near the ports where we were stationed, and beeline to the women. At some ports, like in Barcelona, brothels were located near the shipyards, and it was almost seen as a badge of honour when a guy went with a girl little older than Rae. Not kids, but teens. In the navy, senior officers turned blind eyes to all of it. In Halifax, there were often reports in the newspapers of foreign navy officers assaulting local women in the clubs. But thinking about it then, I wasn't so sure those complaints went anywhere. By and large, guys going off with women — and even girls — wasn't condemned. It was just part of what many men, even those with wives and kids at home, did during their off time.

I reminded myself of all the evidence the police had in Rae's case. There was the photo of her in which she was clearly vomiting, clearly intoxicated and unaware of what was happening to her. Most of all, there was the medical report showing the wounds and the hateful messages which, in themselves, were crimes. "Rae," I said, "the police have more than enough evidence. And you know I've often wondered..." my voice trailed off.

"You wonder what?" Rae probed.

Since the moment I had heard what had happened to Rae, I'd had a nagging feeling that she had been drugged. She was a tall girl, five foot eight and maybe 130 pounds. She blacked out so fast that I couldn't help but suspect someone had slipped her a date-rape drug.

Rae changed the subject. She wanted to return to school, she said. She didn't want to fall behind. She had taken a break from her work with animals, too, and she wanted to return to volunteering at the SPCA. School and the SPCA were really all she had left, she said. She had initially wanted to return to Cole Harbour High, but Leah and I didn't feel that was a good idea. I suggested she come and live with Krista and me and go to Citadel High School, near downtown Halifax, instead. "People don't know you there," I told her.

Rae asked a question then that I couldn't answer: If she didn't do anything wrong, why did she have to go to a different school? Shouldn't the boys go somewhere else? "Why do I have to run?" she asked.

She had me there. "Peanut," I said, using her childhood nickname and picking my words carefully, "your mom and I just want you to be safe. Take some time before going back to school. Start your counselling."

Rae winced then, reminding me how much she had been looking forward to high school. She didn't want to miss the experience. She agreed to take a few more days off but then enroll at Citadel High. If she was leaving Cole Harbour High, though, she wanted to go back one more time and get some art she had been working on. She asked me to accompany her; there were some oil paintings that were half done that she wanted to finish at home. Rae found art a distraction and a balm.

"You got it," I said.

An hour later, Rae and I pulled into our nearest multiplex in my yellow Fiat that Rae and I nicknamed Tweety Bird. The parking lot was already crowded, and Rae looked around and started to breathe heavily. She pulled up the sleeves of her jacket and shirt and started to scratch at her arms. Big, deep scratches, gouging her nails hard into the skin.

For a moment I stared, wondering what she was doing and what I should do. Even in the dim light, I could see her arms turning red. "Don't," I said, leaning over and holding her hands.

"Can we go to another theatre, somewhere farther away, please," she said, almost gasping, out of breath. I could see that her eyes were bug wide, nailed to a group of teenagers on foot, weaving between parked cars. The expression on her face was one of terror, with a furrowed forehead and pinched jaw.

It was the first time I saw that she was deathly afraid of other young people.

A few days later, I drove Rae to Cole Harbour High to pick up her artwork, parking a block away, in plain view of the school's front entrance. Classes were finishing, and students were starting to pour outside, flanking the red-brick building.

Rae had given her phone to Officer Snair at the end of their interview, so she'd had a welcome reprieve from the onslaught of hateful messages and missives from boys asking to date her because, as one wrote, "you put out." Rae and I had made a deal that, when on her laptop, she wouldn't go on Facebook. But if she did, because she was a teenager and curious, she'd forward all messages to Leah or me, and we'd forward them to Officer Snair.

Now that Rae was cut off from the cyberabuse, she wasn't as on edge, expecting each ding or ring to be another fresh wound. In her anxiety's place, though, a melancholy was setting in. Whatever it was surrounding Rae, it made me apprehensive. When she went to her room at night, my chest tightened. I began to check on her, like when she was a child, making sure she was all right. At night, I'd open her door after she had fallen asleep, so I'd wake if she had a nightmare or called out. I didn't trust this darkness that was consuming her; I recognized it in myself, and it scared me.

Rae decided she would go to Dartmouth High School, not Citadel. It was closer to Leah's home, and easier to get to since it didn't require crossing the harbour — no bothering with the city's crowded bridges to visit Leah and her siblings. I took Rae to the mall and bought her new T-shirts, jeans, hoodies, and a jacket. She said she wanted a new beginning, with clothes that didn't remind her of her old school. Despite the dark aura she gave off, she talked about finding hope and meaning in what she was experiencing, a silver lining. She was, she said, trying to emerge. Her clothes were becoming more conservative, like she was trying to hide and redefine herself simultaneously. Years earlier, she had talked about how, for her sixteenth birthday, she wanted a huge party with a DJ who would play Eminem, Lil Wayne, Madonna, and Smashing Pumpkins. She'd wanted to rent out a community centre and invite everyone she knew.

Now, she wanted a quiet dinner at Zen Cuisine, just family.

Rae also wanted to get a tattoo on her birthday. Leah was, at first, against the idea but given what had happened to Rae, we both ultimately gave our permission. Rae presented us both with a solid argument of the symbolism of the tattoo she wanted: a crow's feather. "Feathers are symbols of travel, not just in the physical but also metaphysical world," Rae had told me. "My tattoo represents a break in travel, but a trip far from over."

Rae's favourite purchase was a dark blue hoodie. The colour, she said, reminded her of the ocean, deep down — the unexplored parts where she wanted to dive one day — or the atmosphere, above the ozone layer, high up, the edge of space, just before black. She said the indigo colour made her feel safe, the colour of those places few would ever see.

Some Cole Harbour High students were making their way toward the Fiat, others turning down nearby side streets. Rae slipped down in the seat so she couldn't be seen and held her hands over her head.

"Are you scared?" I asked.

After a short silence, Rae removed her hands and looked over at me. In a calm but serious tone, she asked me if I knew what dark matter was.

I shook my head no.

She then explained that scientists had measured and weighed the universe and our galaxy.

"I didn't know they could do that," I said.

She told me how the mass of what is measurable does not equal what scientists believe to be there. Scientists theorize that much of the universe is comprised of what is known as dark matter, and that this matter provides the gravitational glue that keeps galaxies from tearing themselves apart as they spin their way through the universe. "Scientists don't know too much about dark matter, except that it's all around us. Even maybe here in the car."

Some girls looking about Rae's age, in bomber jackets, Uggs, and ripped jeans giggled past us. Rae poked her head up to look, then slipped back down again.

"Dark matter scares you?" I questioned.

I was expecting Rae to laugh but she didn't. "Yeah, sort of," she said. "What if dark matter are black holes and I'm in one? I can't get out. I can't escape."

"Ah Rae, you can't think like that. What about Gandhi?" Back when Rae was in grade 8, she had learned about Mohandas Gandhi in school. For a while she had become obsessed, wanting to study everything about the Indian revolutionary, including his years in apartheid South Africa as a lawyer. Her password on all her electronics — iPhone, iPad, and laptop — was Gandhi's mantra, "Be the change."

"But people like Gandhi had supporters. I have no one," she whispered. "No one except my family. I don't have any friends anymore." I couldn't even argue. Her friends had stopped calling, except for Antoni and Paul, even those few who had stood up for her initially. After a few moments of silence, she pointed at the school. "Can you go in there?" she asked. "I can't."

As I walked up toward the front door, that sense of sinking that I'd felt the night when I learned what happened to Rae at that party returned. I tried not to, but my eyes moved to the faces of the students I passed. With each one, I asked myself, "Are you the one?" The girl with the pink hair, the nose ring, and the red plaid jacket tied around her waist: "Did you send Rae the message saying you wanted to kill her? Was it you?"

The boys huddled together, laughing conspiratorially, a few wearing school football jerseys, quickly became the naval officers returning from leave and boasting about each other's sexual conquests: "Were you the ones who did this to Rae? Are you the boys congratulating each other for what you did?"

An image came to me then: one so familiar but also very distant, of my father's back, walking up the basement stairs, my hands reaching for him. I felt the plummeting when he didn't turn. This image came to me in very difficult moments, and I never could understand why. But like always when I saw this, my chest felt hot and tight, and I felt short of breath.

"Can I help you?" a voice said, startling me.

I looked up. I was standing in front of the kiosk in the front office. I could feel droplets of sweat dripping down my forehead. I stammered, trying to get my bearings. I squeezed my hands together and swallowed hard, stuffing down the image of my father, the students, my fears. "I came to see the art teacher. My daughter, Rehtaeh Parsons, has some things she needs me to pick up from him."

I felt the woman, a school administrator, looking at me doubtfully. "Are you the one sending Leah messages that my daughter is a slut?" I wanted to ask, the words so close to coming out. Inside, I berated myself for being so paranoid.

I was losing it.

Nothing in that moment seemed rational, and I couldn't understand what was happening to me. This was a high school, a simple high school, but for me as for Rae, it had become a war zone.

"Down the hall and to the right," the administrator replied, her voice friendly and informal. "Can you sign in here?" She pointed to a black binder and a page where others had signed in. As I filled out my name, the date, and the name of the teacher I was visiting, I couldn't stop myself: I scoured the names above mine, wondering whether they could be the boys' parents or the parents of the girls threatening her.

The woman handed me a visitor's pass on a lanyard. "Do you want me to show you the way?" the woman asked when I didn't move.

"No...no," I mumbled, turning slowly. "Thank you for your help."

Once I had rounded a corner and found myself alone, I shifted back against a locker and took long, deep breaths to steady myself. The last thing Rae needed was her father causing a scene in the school and the kids having something else to harass her about.

When I finally made it to the art room, my legs felt like rubber and my body, inside my jacket, was so sweaty that my skin was sticking to my clothes. The art teacher was packing up to leave.

I looked around the room. It was full of colour: paint cans and brushes sat on top of the tables, and the ceramic sink was an artist's pallet of hardened oils. Student artwork hung from pegs on clotheslines stretched from wall to wall. The art teacher, who was maybe fifty years old, small, with thinning grey hair, came up behind me and said hello. His handshake was warm and firm.

"I'm Rehtaeh Parsons's father," I said. "I'm picking up some of her art that she can work on from home."

"I don't understand," he replied after a short pause. "She doesn't go to school here anymore."

"Okay," I said slowly, confused. Rae had only just finalized switching schools. Neither Leah nor I had notified Cole Harbour High that Rae would be withdrawing. "Can I at least get Rae, sorry, Rehtaeh's artwork back?" I finally asked. "It means a lot to her. She wants to work on it at home."

The man shook his head. "When I heard she wasn't returning, I threw out what she was working on."

"What?" Now I was truly baffled.

"I don't have her work," he repeated, raising his hands and shrugging. He was being sincere. He was sorry.

I thanked him and hurried out of the school, forcing myself to not look at anyone. I didn't even hand in my visitor's pass.

When I got back to the car, Rae was playing sudoku on my phone. Seeing me empty-handed, her eyes narrowed and she thrust her bottom lip out, the way she did when she was frustrated or scared. As

I told her what the art teacher had told me, Rae started to wail. She banged her head against the glove compartment and flung her body back and forth, repeating, "I've been erased!" I tried to pull her into my arms to comfort her, but she slapped me away.

Her face was red, her eyes wild and darting.

"People aren't supposed to touch other people's things without their permission," she yelled. It was the first time I heard her say this, but it certainly wouldn't be the last. "It's like people are trying to delete me!"

I finally managed to grab hold of her. I'm a large man, six foot one and over two hundred pounds. Still, using all my force, I found it hard to restrain Rae. But eventually, she slackened. Her wails turned into sobs and she relaxed into my arms. "Dad, that art meant something to me," she mumbled. "People are supposed to respect each other's things. Why do people destroy each other and things that matter?"

Chapter Five

In Nova Scotia, students usually attend schools near their home, within a certain catchment area. And Leah and I just followed the rules, not knowing there were ways around them, so when she queried whether Rae could live at home and attend Dartmouth High, Dartmouth High's guidance department said no. Rae wanted to stay at Leah's, where she could easily meet up with Antoni and Paul. Leah and I felt that their company, as well the closeness of her sisters, Teaghan and Temyson, was critical for Rae's healing. But in the end, Rae's only choices were to return to Cole Harbour High — which now even she was dead set against — or move in with Marianne to attend Dartmouth High. She chose Marianne and Dartmouth.

The day she moved, Rae's mood was somber. I brought her two small suitcases of clothes, as well as some science magazines, books, and a quilt that my mother had made for her, into Marianne's house. Marianne lived in an older house, two storeys tall, painted lime green with white trim. It was in almost the same condition as when it was built in the 1950s. In the back was a garden with abundant wildflowers and ivy spiralling up two oak trees. The house was close to Halifax Harbour, which could be seen from a corner in Marianne's bedroom window, and a cemetery. The staircase to the second floor was tiny, and I had always wondered how Marianne had been able to get the mattresses, the bed frames, and the two large dressers up to the house's two little bedrooms. It was almost like the house had been built around the furniture. The house always struck me as old and stuffy, very much in contrast to Marianne, who was modern and outgoing.

Rae kept her head down the entire time, even to speak. She seemed unable to face me. Her shoulders were rounded, her face long and sagging. Looking back, I knew she was crumbling. She didn't even unpack. She plopped herself down on the couch, pretending to read a book. When I'd peek over her shoulder, I could see she never turned a page.

Not long after I had put her suitcases in her room, Rae announced that she was going to bed. It was just past six o'clock. She said she wasn't hungry, even though Marianne had ordered lemon chicken from Zen Cuisine.

I followed Rae upstairs to give her a new phone I had bought, with a new phone plan and number, so none of her harassers could find her. She didn't open the box. She crawled under the covers and the flannel top sheet with her clothes still on. She didn't even brush her teeth. Rae may have been messy, but she was meticulous about hygiene. I thought her malaise was because we hadn't had any updates from the police.

I left, trying to will myself into believing she would be different — better, happier — once she could throw herself into her studies again. I was wrong.

On her first day, Rae walked to Dartmouth High clutching a thick textbook to her chest. Slung over one arm was her new backpack, which we had picked out together. She was wearing black jeans, her Uggs, a new black bomber jacket, and a dark green scarf knitted by my mother. In my mind's eye she looked much the same as she did at home: head down, so low she kept having to prop up her glasses when they slipped down her nose. I suspected she avoided meeting the gaze of other students, taking in little but their legs and feet: Nike running shoes, high-tops, leather hiking boots, flats, Hunter rain boots, and various Uggs. Jeans, track pants, sweats, the occasional knee-high socks. She had a floor plan that she had splayed out on top of the book she was carrying.

She said later that when she saw the shoes of a pack of girls, tightly wound together, tripping over each other, she headed to the opposite side of the hallway. When she saw boys' shoes, scuffed Adidas and Vans, waves of panic throbbed through her.

In her meeting with Dartmouth High's guidance department the day before, Rae had given her reason for transferring as more diversity in course offerings. The counsellor had remarked that she didn't think Dartmouth offered any courses that Cole Harbour didn't. But she also didn't press Rae for other reasons why she was changing schools. Rae didn't discuss the photograph or the harassment. She simply wanted to forget the bullying, hoping a new school would put it all behind her. Rae took a seat at the back of her homeroom class. Usually she liked to sit at the front, her books spread out in front of her, her hand flying into the air whenever a question was asked.

Now, Rae sat quietly, her books closed, staring forward, avoiding the gaze of the students that she knew were studying her, sizing up the new girl, determining where she would land in the social hierarchy of high school.

Quickly enough she discovered that, despite having been absent from classes for several weeks, Dartmouth's grade 10 math class was at about the place where she had been when she had left Cole Harbour, so she wasn't that far behind. The same in English. They were even reading the same books.

At lunch, she found a nook in a back hall, near a window. She could hear the students talking and shouting in a courtyard below her. She made a mental note to avoid that space: athletes and partygoers. She couldn't eat the tomato sandwich she had made for herself that morning. She took two bites of an apple and tossed the rest uneaten into her paper lunch bag.

She liked school. She liked learning. But it was the in-between stuff that now paralyzed her: walking the hallways to and from classes, lunch, and that time after school when kids linger, gossip, talk, and plan.

She got a text message from Leah partway through her first day, asking if she was doing all right. Rae replied with a thumbs-up emoji. When I texted, she sent me gifs: one of puppies tumbling down a hill and another of kittens leaping out of a box.

She slid through the halls, hoping to be as invisible as dark matter. I imagine her trying to become one of her parallel-universe doppelgängers. But there was no way to communicate between multiverses, she had told me once — no way to transport herself to the universe where what had happened to her hadn't happened, or to solicit help from some wiser, older self.

By day three, Rae felt secure enough that no one at the school knew her or had seen the photograph. She sat a little closer to the front in her classrooms. She even allowed herself to feel excitement that she could finish off the semester. At lunch, she read quotes from the movie *Tree of Life*, a film we'd watched together, which she loved. Her favourite line was: "the nuns taught us there are two ways through life — the way of nature and the way of grace. You have to choose which one you'll follow." Rae told Leah and me that no matter what had happened to her, she vowed she would choose the way of grace, the way of love. Feeling confident, she connected her social-media accounts to her phone, blocking unknown numbers.

Rae made plans to meet up with Antoni and Paul that weekend and do a movie marathon at a theatre downtown, away from Cole Harbour.

She felt good. She felt life returning.

Then, just before the final bell, a message popped up on her phone. It was from a friend of Amanda's. She said she knew that Rae was at Dartmouth High and that she would be waiting out front to beat her up. The girl implied that she was going to send the photo to everyone she knew at Rae's new school and, wherever she went, she would be followed.

Rae looked around the classroom, staring into the faces of the students in her history class, trying to figure out who had told this girl that she was there. The girl in the volleyball uniform, blonde and tall? The boy with curly black hair, who passed notes in class?

Rae quickly stuffed her textbooks and papers into her backpack and hurried from the room, mumbling to the teacher that she had forgotten a doctor's appointment.

Rae headed to the bathroom. Locking herself in a bathroom stall, finding it difficult to breathe, and bent over at the waist with a hand pressed to her chest that felt like it was caving in on itself, she called and texted Leah. "Urgent: come and get me," she said. "It's happened again. The photo…"

Chapter Six

Rae started counselling at the Avalon Sexual Assault Centre, with Leah attending Rae's first session with her. The counselling room felt warm and safe, its cream walls adorned with framed photographs of forest scenes. On one side of the room were stuffed animals and a bookshelf full of titles Rae recognized: *Girl, Interrupted*; *Man's Search for Meaning*; *You Can Heal Your Life*. Renee, Rae's counsellor, said clients could borrow any books they wanted, any time: that it was a library of sorts.

Renee was about fifty, with shoulder-length grey hair and a wide, friendly face. She was slim, short, and wore black-rimmed glasses similar to Rae's. Her voice was soft and calming. When I met Renee, I knew immediately that she and Rae would get along.

Rae was impatient. She wanted to talk about what was happening to her body, about the anxiety and the panic attacks. When she saw other teenagers, particularly in groups, she felt gripped with terror, her pulse racing, her skin perspiring, her body temperature rising, her breathing rapid and raspy. She described the panic attacks as something alien taking over her body, like another person or a thing invading her. She had dreams, too — dreams of the boys, of that night, of waking up, of lights blinding her, the nausea and the flash of a camera. Seemingly anything triggered her: a smell, a voice, a look, the weather, even the ping indicating she had received a message on her phone. Anything could set off the panic.

Rae told Renee that she wanted to be believed. She wanted the boys to apologize, the girls to stop taunting her. She wanted her old life back.

Renee agreed with all that Rae was saying, but stressed the need to do a proper assessment. Renee told Rae she only needed to talk about what she felt comfortable revealing about that night and what had happened at school. Rae talked with Renee about Dartmouth High and the day she got the message, about leaving and not returning. She had moved back in with Leah, making arrangements to return to Marianne's and attend Prince Andrew High School, elsewhere in Dartmouth, after Christmas. Hopefully, she told Renee, by the new year the torment will have stopped.

Renee explained the helplessness, guilt, and shame that sexual assault survivors often felt. She said that what Rae was experiencing with the panic attacks was indeed trauma-related — but they would get through it together. Finally satisfied that she had enough background information, Renee did an exercise in which she had Rae sit back and relax with her eyes closed. She guided Rae through a meditation to find what Renee called Rae's safe place. Rae visualized a field, off of Cole Harbour's Bissett Road, near an old barn and a walking trail where she went with Leah's rescue dogs and the dogs from the SPCA. "Whenever you feel triggered, or when you wake panicked from a dream, go there, in your mind, to your safe place," Renee explained. Eventually, she said, the visualization would become a habit.

That Christmas was one of the best I'd ever had with Rae. Her spirits were buoyed by a call from Detective Constable Snair to Leah, informing us that the police were investigating, and were close to laying charges of sexual assault.

Since starting counselling with Renee, Rae had seemed to settle down a bit and become more focused. The panic attacks were lessening, and she was sleeping through nights with few nightmares. That holiday, we stayed up very late, several nights in a row, watching science-fiction movies, eating Chinese food, and talking about science.

In early 2012, Rae registered at Prince Andrew. At her intake meeting with the school guidance counsellor, she decided to tell the counsellor about the events of November 12, the photograph, the harassment, and the rumours that stalked her to Dartmouth High. Rae asked if the guidance counsellor would be available if she needed help. This time Rae didn't want to be bullied into leaving another school. She wanted to feel safe, join some clubs, meet friends, and graduate. Rae felt that telling the guidance department about her experiences meant the school could be an ally this time.

When the guidance counsellor emerged from that meeting, her face was red and her eyes puffy, Leah told me, whereas Rae glowed. When Rae told me about her meeting with the counsellor, she paraphrased Maya Angelou, in which the author had said there was no greater pain for a person than holding an untold story inside them. Rae told me Renee was helping her tell her story.

Rae explained to me that with Renee's help she was seeing herself as a survivor, not a victim, and that she was starting to feel she could take back control of her life. Rae was using terms like "self care," taking time to eat properly instead of skipping meals, and taking long walks with our dog, Ozzie, in the fresh winter air. A year earlier, Ozzie had come into the SPCA, barely full-grown. For two weeks, he had sat in the shelter waiting for his owner to return, and each day, Rae fell more and more in love, eventually begging me to adopt him. Rae was meeting with Antoni and Paul often, too. I knew they were smoking pot, but it was obvious that it helped to reduce her anxiety and panic attacks. I didn't stop her.

Within the first two weeks of classes, in January 2012, Rae met Chloe, a short, slim, brown-haired teenager with a wide, warm face. The two found themselves sitting beside each other in art class. Chloe had looked over at a picture Rae was sketching and saw her name. She asked Rae where such an interesting name came from.

Rae told her the story: when Leah was a little girl, she drew a card for her cousin Heather, but spelled the name backwards. Everyone had laughed, but not Leah, who said that when she had a little girl, the child would be called Rehtaeh.

Rae had become cautious now of those instant friendships that happen among teenagers, especially teen girls. In her experience, they could often be more about alliances than true affection, and so Rae had turned away, hoping the conversation had ended. But Chloe continued to pepper Rae with questions. What did she like to do? What was her favourite medium to work with in art? And did she like animals because she was drawing one? Not waiting for the answers, Chloe said she liked to watch wildlife documentaries and that struck a chord with Rae, a rare sixteen-year-old girl who followed the release of new David Attenborough films. Chloe explained to Rae that she used reusable stainless-steel cups for her coffee, tried to live a waste-free lifestyle, and wanted to study science. Maybe she *was* a kindred spirit.

In the winter of 2012, Rae seemed happy hanging out with Chloe, and in turn Mandy, Chloe's close friend, and their boyfriends. She even met a boy herself, Blake — tall and lean, with short black hair and freckles. They began dating. All of the girls' boyfriends were older and one had his own loft. Mandy and Chloe would head there on the weekends, Rae and Blake sometimes accompanying them.

The relationship seemed healthy at first. Rae and Blake would go to movies and take walks together. But the longer the relationship went on, the more unhappy Rae seemed. She would return from dates looking like she had been crying. She seemed agitated. Leah and I would ask her what was going on, and she would feign that everything was fine.

Throughout the late winter of 2012, the police were still not reporting much to Leah about the case, despite their pre-Christmas assurances that they were nearing arrests. Rae began to scour the Internet, looking for news reports on Cole Harbour or Eastern Passage boys charged for sexual assault in case the police had just forgotten to let her and Leah know. She daydreamed of the day the police would call to confirm the boys had been arrested and the photograph confiscated. "It's over" was what she wanted to hear from the police. She imagined that day would feel like a door opening to a new life.

And then the blows started to rain down again. Renee was let go from the Avalon Sexual Assault Centre, which had to trim its budget — Renee, with the least seniority, was the first to leave. Since December she'd been a beacon for Rae, and now she was gone.

Then, within the first few weeks of March, Officer Snair left a voice message on Leah's phone saying that the police now had evidence. Rae interpreted that as a good sign; the police were narrowing in on the boys. But when Leah tried to call Officer Snair back to learn what this evidence was, she always got her voicemail. Officer Snair never returned the call to elaborate.

Rae tried to keep up with the meditations and visualizations she had learned with Renee and agreed to meet with a new therapist. But she walked out halfway through the session, feeling uncomfortable retelling her story, like she was backtracking.

But the final blow was seeing the boys and her former friends on social media: they posted pictures of sports events and parties, like nothing had ever happened. The girls too, including Amanda, seemed to have just moved on with life. Rae found it increasingly difficult to stay optimistic. She started skipping classes and tests, smoking weed instead with Chloe and Mandy.

"Karma," she told me one day. "I must have bad karma. Maybe I did something horrible in a past life so I'm paying for it in this life."

"I don't think karma works like that," I told her. "And you have no such thing."

Rae sighed. She was doubting herself more often now, she said — more often than believing herself. She told me that she was beginning to believe the bad in the world absorbed all the light and hope from the rest: an emotional black hole.

I wanted Rae to be wrong. I wanted her to see the mystery and beauty in the world the way she had as a child. I told her I was worried she was studying black holes too much. I suggested she try and balance what she was learning, reminding her what she herself had said about the world of quantum physics: "scientists know so little." I reminded her of the times she spent with animals as a small child, when she would say to me afterwards what it was like time had stopped, and she could hear their tiny heartbeats as if she and they were one. I wanted her to find that peace again.

One day, after smoking under a bridge with Chloe, Rae learned of another girl, Tiffany, who had allegedly been assaulted by one of the boys. Rae found the girl's number and texted her to see if she'd like to meet.

When Rae told me about Tiffany, she looked at me with bright eyes: "I'm not alone anymore." There were other girls like her, as sad as that was, she told me, but now the police could get the boys. Rae felt there was no way the police could move slowly now. They would have to act fast to protect anyone else.

Chapter Seven

Rae studied Tiffany as she walked toward her: dark hair, a childlike face, large brown eyes. Rae felt a connection in that gaze, mutual understanding: it had happened to her too.

Still, Rae's guard was up. She wondered whether she was for real, or whether this was a trick; a plant by one of the girls who had threatened to expose her, hurt her, beat her up.

Tiffany began. Rae told me that Tiffany said that Cole Harbour High wasn't doing anything to stop the photo from being circulated. Rae told her she thought the police had gone to the school and interviewed students, but Tiffany told Rae that the police didn't seem to be doing anything about the boys.

Rae changed the subject, recounting to Tiffany the story that she had been told and had later relayed to me. How one night, as Tiffany walked home, this boy pulled her into a shed, muffling her mouth with his hand so roughly she had bruises she had to cover with foundation for days afterwards. At this point in the telling Tiffany began crying. Rae asked whether she reported it to the police, and Tiffany told her she hadn't. In fact, Tiffany then got angry at Rae, saying that these were all rumours: nothing had happened to her. She wasn't assaulted. It was all a lie.

I picked Rae up. She was standing under a tunnel near a park. She was sopping wet, her hair stringy, her eyes drooping and glossy. She had never looked so deflated, I thought, dragging her feet, her shoulders sagging. As she moved toward the car, the rain now a torrent, Rae looked more lost than I had ever seen her.

That night, Rae briefly perked up and, for the first time, took control of speaking with the police. She was tired of the back-and-forth phone messages between Detective Constable Snair and her mother. She wanted to know dates: when the police went into the school, as they promised they would, and stopped the circulation of the photograph. She wanted to know when the boys would be charged, and didn't want to accept "we're working on it" or "we're close." She wanted to know what evidence Officer Snair was referring to in the last voice message to Leah about now having evidence. Most of all, she wanted the police to know there were other victims.

Rae called, but Officer Snair didn't pick up, and Rae had to leave a message.

That Friday, still with no response from the police, Rae felt she was no further along in her recovery than the first few days after that night. She had no real faith left that the police were going to help her.

She blew off a math test and smoked some weed with Chloe. On her way out of school, Rae got a text message from Blake, asking her to call him. She did. He said he'd seen the photograph. Someone had sent it to him, but he wouldn't tell Rae who. He said he wanted to take a break from their relationship, that he didn't believe Rae was assaulted, and that he believed the rumours that Rae enjoyed having sex with lots of boys. He questioned whether Rae knew what it meant to be faithful. Rae begged to talk about the break-up in person, to explain the photograph, but Blake wouldn't listen and didn't want to meet. After he hung up, he ghosted, not responding to any of Rae's voice messages or texts.

She walked away from school without Chloe, which she never did. She found her way to Marianne's house, where she knew she'd be alone since her aunt was teaching that afternoon. Rae walked into the tiny living room wearing her Uggs, muddy from the spring thaw.

Her mind was spinning again, bursting with fresh and awful thoughts. Later she could only describe their colour: red and black. She scratched her arms until she drew blood.

On wobbly legs she moved up the slim staircase to Marianne's room. She found Marianne's black dress belt. All she wanted in this moment was for the ugly thoughts and hopelessness to end. She tightened the belt around her neck.

As she wrote in her diary, "I am drowning in a black hole." Then she admitted that the words she told herself, that she now believed were true, were the words that had been told to her.

Sluts are not welcome here.

Rehtaeh Parsons is good for one thing only: a gangbang.

Loser, whore...die Rehtaeh. Die. Why don't you just go and kill yourself. Your life is nothing more than a rag anyways.

Chapter Eight

Excerpt from the authors' interview with Chloe (winter 2019):

She just disappeared, you know. Rae. She was there one day at school, and then vanished the next.

We met in art class. She was sketching a black and white drawing of an animal. I don't remember which kind. Rae and I both loved animals and drew them: bears, dogs, dolphins. I kept looking over at her art because it was really good. I hadn't seen her before at school, and of course everyone is curious about the new girl. But she seemed like she had a wall around her. I could just sense she didn't want to talk. She looked like the friendly type, you know, but then when I approached her she was so closed off. She signed her name at the bottom and that's when I just went for it. She seemed interesting to me. She seemed like she was in her own world, or two places at once. I dunno.

I told her she had a cool name and asked her how she pronounced it.

Without looking up, she mumbled something. I couldn't hear her.

I took a guess and I guess I pronounced it right, because she looked up then and nodded.

She then went back to her drawing.

I asked her where she got her name. She said it was Heather spelled backwards and explained where her mom got the name from.

I asked her to go for lunch with me and she agreed. She was shy and we talked mostly about animals: animal rescues, the oceans and what a mess they were, animal and wildlife documentaries. We liked the same shows and the same things.

I knew she was carrying with her some baggage but I didn't ask. Not long after we had become friends, a guy told me a bit of her story. We were driving — myself, a few girls, and some guys. This particular guy, sitting in the front seat, had leaned over and said to me in the backseat, "You know there is a picture of that girl you're hanging out with, a picture of her going around having sex." I didn't ask for more details. I didn't care. Gossip in high school is like radio waves, constantly coming at you. I'd had enough of people talking about me, saying I wasn't a good girl, I did drugs, I skipped, you know.

Rae, my best friend Mandy, and I slipped into an easy friendship. High, we'd watch animal documentaries — anything narrated by Morgan Freeman and Sir David Attenborough. I'd drink rum, Rae might have a beer, but mostly we liked weed. She wasn't a big drinker. We'd meet before school. We'd hang out at lunch. I was her only friend for a long while, until she warmed up to Mandy too. Rae seemed to like it being us three. And the guys, our boyfriends. Mandy and I dated older guys who got the booze and weed for us. We'd hang out at Mandy's boyfriend's loft, smoking and laughing. I could tell Rae was sad about something and weed made her feel better.

I was with her, with her a few times, when a girl would come up to us and want to fight. Once was at a Tim

Hortons where we were having coffee. Another time was at school. Rae would raise her arms above her head and just stare out. She was always taller than her attackers, so that stance was like she was trying to just ignore them.

I wanted to know, to know the whole story, but I also felt I was a safe place for her, a place for Rae to forget, so I waited for her to feel comfortable enough to tell me.

Then she just disappeared. One day, we were meeting up before school like we always did, like she was scared to go down the hallways on her own; the next day, gone.

March 24, 2012: Marianne had a feeling, she told me, when she entered the house. Her eyes immediately moved to the muddy footprints ascending the stairs. She followed them up almost against her will, and when she arrived on the landing and saw the overhead light of the guest room — Rae's room — snaking its way into the hallway, she knew.

She pushed open the door and saw her own black belt hanging from the overhead light fixture. Then she heard sobs and soft moaning coming from a corner of the room. Marianne turned slowly, afraid of what she was about to see, to find her niece sitting with her legs tucked into her chest, her head down, her hands clasped tightly to her ears like she was trying to block out some sound.

Marianne exhaled then and fell to her knees. She crawled to Rae, pulling her into a tight embrace.

"I didn't want to do it," Rae mumbled, letting her body fall onto Marianne's. "I just wanted the nightmare to stop. The noise in my head."

Marianne bundled Rae up in a wool blanket and moved her downstairs to the couch in the tiny living room on the first floor.

As she called me to come over, Marianne boiled water for tea.

As soon as I arrived at Marianne's house, Rae begged me to have her admitted to a mental-health facility for teens. "I want to live, Dad," she told me. "I want to get better. I need help." She pushed her iPhone toward me and had me look at a site she'd brought up, for Halifax's IWK Health Centre and its crisis programs for youth. As I read the information, Rae tapped her bare feet. Before I could finish reading, she grabbed the phone back and had me look at another site. This one listed signs of psychological trauma: thoughts of suicide, distorted or psychotic thinking, intense anxiety, depression, the inability to cope.

Rae stood and started to pace, her cheeks flushed, her eyes wild, and her hands gesturing frantically as she spoke. She was remarkably self-possessed and clear-eyed about what was happening to her — not just the lingering trauma, but the impossibility of healing as long as that photograph was circulating and her harassers were free to torture her. She likened it to a wound being torn open again and again: "Stab, stab, stab," she motioned with her hand.

That night, I took her to the emergency department at the IWK. She had packed a suitcase — full of school work, since she expected to be admitted for several weeks — along with clothes, toiletries, and a few stuffed animals that, even as a teenager, brought her comfort. I was asked to leave about midnight, to return in the morning to discuss the plan for Rae.

I thought our morning meeting would be with Rae, a psychiatrist, and me, and we would be having her inpatient consultation. I was expecting that we would be talking about the course of therapy for Rae. During the night, Rae had been moved to 4 South, the youth mental-health facility.

When I reached 4 South, I had to be signed in by a nurse at the triage desk. Next, I had to move through a series of metal detectors. Finally, free and clear, I was buzzed into a locked hallway.

The ward for youth mental health spanned one part of one floor of the hospital and was divided into sections depending on the needs of the kids in care; 4 South was for patients deemed most at risk. In 4 South, kids are locked in and the public locked out, except for immediate family and guardians, so that staff can work without distraction. It was exactly what Rae believed she needed.

I followed a nurse down a long hallway lined by doors, most of them shut but a few open. I glanced inside those left ajar, wanting to see rooms like the one Rae would call home, and the kids she'd be living among. In one, my eyes locked with those of a tiny girl, just a child, maybe ten. She was sitting on her bed, her legs stretched over the side. A woman, sitting on a chair in front of the child, was stroking her hand, while a man was shaking his head. "But I want to go home for the weekend, you promised I could come home," the girl said, looking up and catching my eye. I looked away, just as the woman said, "You're not ready yet."

The nurse I was trailing finally stopped in front of an office, turned to me, and pointed inside. In a gruff voice, she said, "The nurse will meet you here." I was taken aback. I assumed I'd be meeting Rae's doctor. I was further shocked when I entered the office — it was nothing like the counselling rooms at the Avalon Sexual Assault Centre. The ambience here was sterile and industrial: white walls, silver fixtures, fluorescent lighting, with the windows all covered on the outside by chain mesh.

As I walked into the office, the nurse turned to leave. "And my daughter?" I asked. The nurse paused but didn't turn to look. "Where's my daughter?" I asked again.

"Who is your daughter?" she asked.

"Rehtaeh Parsons. I signed in."

"I'll find her," she said briskly, and then left.

I sat for about five minutes until Rae meandered in, lifeless, dragging her feet, bringing with her a breeze of hospital smells: cleaning agents and processed food. She slumped her body down into the chair beside me, her hands drooping over the armrests. "What have they given you?" I leaned over and asked.

Groggily, slurring her words and speaking almost in slow motion, she explained: "Lorazepam, or something like that."

A different nurse, short with cropped black hair greying at the temples, entered the office. She was middle-aged, stressed-looking. Her eyes were half-moons, heavy and tired.

Rae, with a long sigh, sank even further down into her chair.

"So I want to go over the plan this morning," the nurse said.

"Yes, yes," I piped up, my back stiffening, eager to get on with things. I started to explain to the nurse that terrible night, the bullying, how Rae was so confident and driven before, but was now a different person. She needed to find her way back to who she was. I was barrelling forward when the nurse put her hand up and told me to stop.

"I want to know if Rae has a plan, a suicide plan," she said, matter-of-factly. "Kids often devise their plan and try many times."

My mouth hung open and I stared unblinking at the nurse. "Of course Rae doesn't have a plan," I finally said. "She's been harassed to the point she can't stay in one school without fearing for her physical safety. The police keep saying they are near to laying charges and then we wait and wait and wait." All of this was out of my mouth when Rae interrupted me.

"Yes, I have a plan."

I gasped and turned to look at her. Her face was sallow and her eyes downcast.

"What is your plan, Rehtaeh?" the nurse asked.

"With a belt. Hanging. But I don't really want to," she said slowly, her words falling from her lips like bubbles. "I wake up and all I feel is darkness. Sleep is the only place I feel safe. It's like I wake up into a nightmare and I want the nightmare to stop." Tears pooled in both my eyes and Rae's, hers dripping down her cheeks.

"How long will she need to stay?" I heard myself asking. "Can we discuss the course of treatment? At Avalon, Rae was doing trauma therapies."

What Rae wanted, and what I wanted for her, was trauma-informed therapy, which focuses on recognizing triggers of the initial traumatic episode. It is conducted with therapists familiar with the complexity of psychological trauma and aware of their patients' fragility and sensitivity. Rae had started these therapies with Renee, I told the nurse. "It should not be difficult to pick up the therapy from where Rae and Renee had left off."

The nurse's eyes moved from Rae's to mine and then back again. "We're sending Rehtaeh home," she finally said. "That's why you're here: to talk about Rehtaeh's release plan."

My eyes widened like saucers. For a moment, I wondered if I had heard incorrectly. The nurse looked down and began writing some notes in a file. Her face was serious, severe, like the nurse who had led me to this office.

"I think there's been some mistake," I eventually spluttered.

The nurse shook her head and shuffled some papers. She asked to be excused for a moment so she could check on something.

She was only gone a few minutes, but in that time, Rae lifted her heavy head and our eyes locked. "Dad, if I leave here, I will die," she whispered.

The nurse returned. "Yes, we're sending Rehtaeh home," she said. "I've got the release papers."

"I'm not signing any forms releasing Rae... Rehtaeh. She tried to kill herself yesterday," I pressed, as the nurse sat back down behind her desk. "She had a counsellor, a good counsellor, at the Avalon Sexual Assault Centre, who was let go. Rae needs help. I thought we were going over her plan of treatment." As I spoke, my anger grew. My temples throbbed and, under the table, my legs were shaking.

"Can she leave with you?" The nurse pushed a hospital document toward me, like she hadn't heard a word I said.

I shook my head and folded my arms across my chest. "I told you. I am not signing any release..."

"I do drugs," Rae cut in. "I have an addiction problem."

"Heroin?" the nurse said, cocking an eyebrow and swivelling her head to look at Rae.

"Yes, I do heroin," Rae said. She was now looking up and while her body was trembling, likely from the medication she was on, she was trying to pull herself up straight.

"Cocaine?" the nurse asked next.

"Uh-huh. And crystal meth...I use MDMA, too. Oh, and crack," said Rae.

I swallowed hard, a knot forming in my chest. What was I missing?

"Alcohol too," Rae said. "Whisky." I had never in my life smelled hard liquor on Rae. And I knew enough from my brother Casey what heavy alcohol use looks and smells like.

"Why did you say all that stuff about using drugs and drinking whisky?" I asked when Rae and I were alone in her room. The nurse, after the discussion around drugs, had agreed to admit Rae to 4 South for an indefinite period of time.

"Because I had read online that a lot of the treatment programs here were focused on drugs and alcohol abuse," she said, sitting down on her bed and looking around the room. It was sparsely furnished: a bed, a brown paper bag for garbage, a desk bolted to the ground, a chair. Rae was told she could decorate the walls, which were white. I shivered, thinking how the hospital reminded me of the isolation wards in mental institutions I had seen in movies. Even the window looked like the window of a prison.

"I thought the nurse would take me more seriously if she knew I had an addiction," Rae continued. I put her backpack filled with art supplies and books on the floor, and her small duffle bag of clothes in the closet for her to unpack when she was ready.

"Dad," she whispered. I looked over at Rae, who was staring out the window. "If they release me, I will die," she repeated. "If I go home, I will be dead. You know that? I had to say what I had to say."

"Yes," I murmured, hoping she would get the care she needed, even though I had a nagging feeling that what Rae needed was to get the hell out of there. I just chalked up my apprehension to the distrust I now had of any system — the police, the school — to help Rae. The hospital, I convinced myself as I left, would be different.

Chapter Nine

Direction given by writer...for PT (Patient) to remove clothing...and safety smock to be put on. PT made crude comments regarding staff wanting PT to strip and see her naked. PT began taking off clothes...security presence required. PT stated: "What are these men doing here? They just want to see me naked. I am 16. How old are they? Like 50. This is illegal."

— Excerpt from Rehtaeh Parsons's 4 South psychiatric file

For the first few days Rae was in 4 South, she had to remain in her room, including for meals. Those on the ward with eating disorders had their bathroom doors locked by staff for an hour after each meal to ensure that they didn't purge their food. The staff was uncertain of Rae's food habits, so they locked her bathroom too and checked that she'd eaten all her food. Of all the things going on with Rae, an eating disorder was not one of them. Once Rae had settled in and had the go-ahead from staff, she was permitted to take part in group programs and visit the lounge on the floor below, where there was a pool table and arts-and-crafts supplies. But after a couple of weeks in the hospital, I felt there was still no change in Rae. Actually, I sensed she was getting worse, and I wasn't surprised. The system at 4 South seemed set up for youth with extreme discipline problems and, as Rae had noted, addictions. To me the environment seemed punitive and disciplinarian, the opposite of the supportive and caring environment she needed.

Rae told me she had started to cut herself, which had not really happened prior to admission, as far as I knew. Rae said she used the zipper of her jeans to scratch her wrists and then moved on to paper clips she would steal from the nurses and the balls of pens. She showed me her hacked-up arms.

She told me the physical pain diverted her thoughts, which were otherwise consumed by the memories of that night, messages people had sent to her, the girls threatening to beat her up, and the photograph. "Watching the blood come out is like watching the pain leave," she told me. Rae said she hadn't learned to cut from the other girls in the ward who did. She'd already known about cutting and, in fact, digging her nails into her skin when she had her panic attacks was just a precursor of what was to come. But it only progressed to this degree during her stay at the IWK, and this was one of the clearest indicators of how her treatment seemed to leave her worse off. It had become a game — so many kids were cutting on 4 South that the staff were forever confiscating anything that could be used to do so. Cutting on the floor seemed, from what Rae told me, to be a small act of rebellion on the part of the youth against the nurses and doctors.

At the hospital, Rae was taking what she could from the various programs. The psychologists and psychiatrists she spoke with focused on her attempted suicide and anxiety, but not, it seemed, the root causes. Rae enjoyed the group classes of art therapy, where she made stuffed animals and clay figurines. In her group therapy sessions, the other patients talked about their drug abuse. Rae wanted to talk about what had happened to her and its aftermath.

I was visiting Rae every day, and I began suggesting that maybe she should come home. I would take a leave of absence from my job at the Apple Store and stay with her. But she was still afraid. She described the mental-health system as useless, entirely focused on drug and alcohol addictions, but she still couldn't think about leaving. She said that her days before the hospital were dark, stormy, even the brightest ones grey and dismal. She felt like she was sinking deeper with each breath into a black hole. Whenever she began to feel she was back among the living, that sense of being alive would be punctured somehow: a text message, a comment online from someone telling her to die or that she deserved to be raped, or a girl wanting to beat her up. Rae didn't want to go back to that life, even though the hospital didn't seem much better.

Rae did enjoy the field trips to the Halifax Junior Bengal Lancers, a horse-riding school nearby that hosted a therapeutic riding program. This was where the hospital seemed innovative, Rae told me, even forward-thinking. Animal therapy of this kind has been strongly associated with reduced stress and improved self-esteem, and there's something to be said for helping those who feel vulnerable to remember there are creatures in the world even more in need of help than they are.

But those moments of calm for Rae were few and far between.

Rae knew, through whispered conversations, that most of the girls on the ward had suffered a sexual assault, somewhere, sometime. A relative, a friend, a stranger. The girls would huddle together when they could, when staff wasn't looking. Rae told me that the girls mostly talked about their lives and the people who had hurt them. The girls said they felt afraid on the co-ed ward. Even if the counsellors had wanted to talk about sexual violence in the group sessions, the girls told one another, they were too afraid to discuss their experiences in front of the guys.

Rae enjoyed getting to know some of the other girls on the ward, including Molly, a frail and emaciated girl who said she was in for cutting and depression. Rae became almost a champion of the weaker girls, watching out for them, telling new arrivals the rules — like not to wear short sleeves, because staff didn't like kids showing each other their wounds from cutting.

Molly and Rae did art together, giggled about the dragon portrait in the hospital's lobby, and spoke about their own traumas.

The kids on the ward, Rae explained, played games like Lorazepam Hour. An anti-anxiety medication, one of its side effects was fatigue. Rae told me that the kids would compete to see who could stay awake the longest.

About a month after Rae was admitted, I arrived one morning to find her throwing her clothes around the room and ripping up the pictures of goblins and the black-and-white sketches of animals she had done and taped to her wall. I had had no warning she was upset. No one from the hospital had called to inform me.

With her arms flailing, her eyes wild, she explained that she was caught standing up for Molly. A new patient had pushed Molly to go away, feigning she was an old friend of Rae's. Rae had snapped at the new patient to get lost: "I don't know you." As punishment, Rae had been banned from the recreation room and her own art supplies from home were confiscated.

Rae was so hard to console — screaming that the rules were unfair and that the nurses weren't hearing her and the other girls and what they needed to heal — that I called out for help. I wanted a psychiatric nurse to assist me in settling her down.

I told the nurse who arrived and stood in the doorframe the story Rae had recounted for me, and all the while Rae was pacing, digging her nails deep into her legs. "It's just another day in my personal hell, Dad," she spat out.

"You know, you don't have to take this," the nurse said to me.

My eyes flew from Rae to the nurse. I hadn't heard right. Surely, this woman didn't just say that?

"You don't have to put up with this," the nurse repeated.

I stumbled backwards, dumbfounded, until I was sitting on Rae's bed.

Rae stopped pacing and stared at me, pushing her bottom lip out. I stared back at her through teary eyes.

As a father, as a man, I have never felt so helpless as I did in that moment. I was supposed to be the caregiver for this family; that was my role, to provide safety for my child. I was failing, and that failure filled me with guilt, anger, and fear of the unknown. I didn't know what to do. Rae reiterated that she would die if she left.

I feared she was going to die staying.

After nearly a month in the hospital, Rae was allowed to leave to visit her family. She saw Leah and then went to Marianne's house and arrived back on the 4 South ward at 7:10 p.m.

The nurse asked if Rae had cut while she was out on her pass. Rae admitted she had, with a slim blade she had pulled from a Bic razor. Rae was so vulnerable at this point that anything could trigger her panic. She told the nurse that after finding some of Blake's clothes in her closet at home, she had become sad and anxious, worried that she would never find love again and that she would always be judged by that photograph. After she found Blake's clothes, she texted him to tell him that she missed him. He didn't reply. That's when she went to the bathroom to cut. When she emerged, she had an argument with Leah over money. Rae said she wanted to buy some weed but was broke. Leah told her no. Rae had left in a huff, taking the bus to Marianne's house, hoping it would be a place to relax.

Rae lifted the sleeves of her hoodie for the nurse, revealing the wounds: some clotted, dark, purply-red bubbles; others raw, scraped skin. "The feeling of betrayal… that no matter what I do I can't outrun that night… I can't cope… the noise in my head, you know," Rae explained, as the nurse scribbled notes in her file.

The nurse looked up and asked if Rae would allow a hazard check. Rae nodded. She knew what a hazard check was from her trips to the horse stables. She would be searched for contraband, drugs, or sharp items, first by walking through the metal detector and then by allowing a security guard to run a hand-held detector over her

body. The clasps on her bra beeped. The nurse said she would have to
inspect more closely and asked to follow Rae to her room.

Once in her room, Rae pulled up her shirt and gave permission
for the nurse to search inside her bra. The nurse patted down Rae's
body, removing her iPod from the hoodie pocket and the slim digital
camera that I had given her for Christmas from her hip pocket.

After the security check reported that she was clean, Rae went to
the recreation room and played some pool by herself. I had taught
Rae how to shoot when she was little, at a billiards place not far from
Leah's house.

Rae was enjoying herself, she told me afterwards. She thought
back to her afternoon at Marianne's, drifting around the backyard
in the spring sun, listening to the sounds of birds, the distant roar of
the sea (which her aunt said was impossible to hear from the house,
though Rae insisted she could). By the late afternoon, Rae was feeling
good about things again, calmer, a little hopeful about life. Sitting in
the backyard, she said that she inhaled the beauty of the world that
once moved her: the scents of freshly cut grass, spicy warm lilac from
a nearby tree, and wet earth.

In the recreation room, a boy meandered over to Rae just as she
was about to take a shot. He said something to her that made her
jump and miss the ball. She swore, then turned and glared at him. He
was wiry, tall, long limbed and ginger haired, with acne on his cheeks.
He was agitated, shifting from foot to foot, his eyes darting back and
forth. He began flicking his fingers.

Rae tried to catch his eyes, shaking her head, trying to motion to
him not to talk to her, to go away, to leave her alone. But he wouldn't
look at her. He kept rambling on about a girl he knew, who had just
died by suicide. He made reference, Rae told me, to photographs
of the girl naked that were sent around, saying loose girls like her
deserved to die.

Rae's skin temperature rose.

Her face became flushed, her eyes watered, her chest contracted.

She told me it felt like an apple had lodged itself in the back of her throat and she struggled to breathe: the usual precursors to a panic attack.

The boy continued talking, almost a rant, saying girls like her were messed up. Rae cupped the palms of her hands over her ears and shook her head wildly. The boy didn't seem to register her distress.

Rae started to cry, large droplets of tears stinging her chapped lips. The boy talked about a party, getting drunk, having sex, like this was what he wanted to do with Rae.

The noise, the static, moving in and around Rae's head, and the sinking pain bearing down on her chest, made her start to rock from foot to foot. Eyes closed, she kept telling the boy to stop.

Then her eyes popped open, she swore, and then she shouted, "You have no right to speak to me that way!"

A nurse rushed over and shushed her to calm down. The boy, still talking, moved off.

Rae threw her pool stick on the table. "Call my mom," she yelled. Rae peeled herself away from the nurse who was holding her arm. "Tell my mom that I am going to kill myself tonight," she yelled as she stormed out of the recreation room.

According to her medical file, at 11:30 p.m., Rae emerged from her room, staggering and wearing dark sunglasses. She announced that she had smuggled in ecstasy pills inside her bra; a bra that staff had already checked and in which they'd found nothing.

She boasted that she had taken the pills.

Rae was ordered to take off the glasses and asked if she would go to the isolation room. Rae said yes.

A pediatrician, an on-call resident, and a nurse escorted Rae to the room. There was nothing inside but a slim mattress and a pillow, and a single bare bulb overhead.

The hospital staff locked Rae inside and left.

Not long after, Rae started tearing the mattress apart, ripping the seams of the fabric and throwing what she could pull off against the wall. At 1:30 a.m., still in the isolation room, Rae threw some cheese and crackers she was given to eat against the wall. A nurse checked her vital signs. Rae's pulse was elevated. She was given Lorazepam to help calm her down.

At 2:15 a.m., Rae removed her tank top and ripped apart more of the mattress. At 3 a.m., she took off her pants and draped them around her neck like a scarf. She was hot, she told me later. The room had no air circulation. She felt itchy from the heat, and sweaty. Most of all, she told me, she felt confined, imprisoned, choked.

At 3:45 a.m., a nurse entered the room with two security guards and asked Rae to remove the rest of her clothes and wear a medical smock. Rae cursed and yelled: "What are these men doing here? They just want to see me naked. I am 16. How old are they?" She then asked for the hospital to call me. "My dad would not allow this," she shouted.

The nurse told Rae she could call me when she had calmed down. The nurse reiterated that what they were doing was for her own "medical safety." Rae cursed again and called out for a lawyer: "I have rights, you know."

With the staff not bending to her wishes, Rae eventually murmured, "I want to die. I want to die."

The nurse asked Rae to lie down on her stomach. Rae did what was asked. The nurse gave her a needle of Lorazepam in her buttocks.

Rae settled down for a bit after that. She told me she drifted into a fitful, muddied sleep: faces of strange people and beings jumped up in front of her; disjointed scenes appeared that were so vivid she thought them real, including seeing me die. She wasn't even sure she was awake when something made her bolt upright. She remembered hurling herself toward the wall and kicking it. She pounded on the door with her fists to be let out, her dry, scratchy voice calling for help.

When no one came to help her, she shouted, "I will fucking kill everybody!"

Rae left the isolation room at 8:43 a.m. Her hospital file says that she was placed in the room because of the narcotics she'd taken the night before, which made her "agitated and she needed to settle."

Rae left the facility not long after that incident. By then, she wanted to leave too, promising that she was going to do her healing on her own.

Her release records stated she had "adjustment disorder with depressed mood and disturbance of conduct and substance abuse disorder." The file also noted "academic decline, unsatisfactory heterosexual relations with marked conflict, poor peer relations and history of sexual abuse."

A history of sexual abuse? This was the last written comment in Rae's file — almost, it seemed to me, an afterthought.

Chapter Ten

After the hospital, Rae came to live with Krista and me. We lived in a three-storey, canary-yellow townhouse in Armdale, a quiet neighbourhood separated from Halifax's downtown peninsula by a narrow inlet called the Northwest Arm.

Armdale felt far from Cole Harbour, on the other side of the city and far enough away that Rae could walk around with little risk of running into anyone she knew. She was back in counselling at the Avalon Sexual Assault Centre, although she still found it difficult to bond with any of the therapists the way she had with Renee. Staff at 4 South had given us referrals to day and group programs, but the first one Rae attended saw her sitting directly across from a boy she recognized from Cole Harbour High. When their eyes locked, Rae said, he smirked. She bolted from the room, and thereafter refused to attend anything recommended by the IWK. "They're a joke," she texted me on the bus ride home.

Rae took a part-time job at a dog daycare. Being around animals, she believed, helped her more than any counselling program she'd attended, except for her time with Renee. In her own time, she kept up the meditation exercises Renee had taught her. She cut off most communication with her friends, except to smoke pot with Antoni and Paul. She had me take her to the Halifax Shambhala Centre, a Buddhist institute, where she picked up literature on mindfulness.

In her research on trauma, Rae landed on a Vancouver doctor named Gabor Maté, who had worked with residents of that city's Downtown Eastside, one of the poorest neighbourhoods in Canada, full of residents dealing with addictions and unresolved trauma. Rae had Leah and me look into whether there were any therapists in the Halifax area that offered similar trauma therapies. There were few discoverable mental-health programs for teens, whether they suffered from eating disorders, cutting, drug use, or sexual violence, and those that were available had long waiting lists. They were also run by private psychologists and would not be covered by my health insurance from the navy, which provided only $1,000 in any fiscal year for mental-health services. These therapists were charging as much as $350 a session. We all knew that Rae needed sustained therapy, perhaps several sessions per week. Neither Krista and I nor Leah could afford the thousands of dollars needed for private care.

Rae told Leah and me that rape seemed to be the trauma, the betrayal, the loss of self that led these girls to their addictions and mental-health issues. She said that if she had millions of dollars, she would open a mental-health centre for teenagers. Leah and I promised we would keep searching for a program for Rae. While she waited, Rae improved her diet, exercised, prayed, and meditated. She even got Leah's permission to get a tattoo on her arm: "Strength and Courage" written in Japanese characters. Rae said the tattoo was a way of reclaiming her own body after what had been done to it, to her.

But every time she seemed to be doing well, something out of her control came crashing down. In the spring and early summer of 2012, Blake started texting Rae again, calling her a slut and telling her that no one would want her, that she was worthless. I don't know what prompted this increase in abuse, but one night Rae cut so deeply that her sheets were covered in blood. I bandaged her up and rocked her. The wounds weren't deep enough for us to go to the hospital, but they were terrifying. And there was no way, until Leah and I found a therapist who could handle Rae's case the way she needed, that I was admitting her to a mental-health facility again.

Rae was desperate for an update from the police. She wanted to return to school in September and hoped that by then the harassment would have stopped. But by mid-July, there was still no word from Detective Constable Snair, and a liaison worker with the Avalon Sexual Assault Centre suggested to Leah that we arrange a sit-down meeting with the police. "I doubt the police will tell you much," the liaison worker said, "but at the least they'll know you're still out there."

In early August 2012, Leah, Rae, the liaison worker, and I went to the Halifax Regional Police's East Division headquarters in Dartmouth, where we were shuffled into a boardroom for a meeting with Officer Snair and her supervisor, Sergeant Ron Legere. Officer Snair arrived with a stack of files and took charge of the meeting, while Sergeant Legere, who didn't say much, nodded. Later I would wonder if he was there to ensure that his protégé was doing things by the book and that we couldn't find grounds to file a complaint.

The room was bright and hot, flanked by tall windows, and Leah fanned her face with a pamphlet.

Leah's first question was about whether the police had the boys' cellphones and computers. Had the police traced who had taken the picture and charged them with child pornography, as they had suggested they would do eight months earlier? Officer Snair, shuffling some notes from the files, eventually replied that she was waiting for the warrants to come in for the boys' phones and computers.

"But it's been nine months," I said, sitting up and moving forward. "Warrants don't usually take that long to execute, correct?"

Rae, sitting between Leah and me, started to fidget, playing with a paperclip and shifting back and forth in her chair.

I don't recall Officer Snair's response: something like, it's just the way it was in this case.

"Did you bring the boys in?" I asked. "Find out from them directly what happened that night? Did you bring the boys in, separate them, and interview them one by one?"

Officer Snair grew testy, then, accusing me of telling her how to do her job. I sighed and leaned back. The Avalon liaison was right. "This meeting is a waste of time," I mumbled.

Leah let out a frustrated laugh and Rae started to breathe heavily, like she was about to have a panic attack. "Why did you give me hope that you were close to laying arrests?" she exclaimed. I looked over at her. She was staring at the ceiling, trying to block off tears.

The Avalon worker cut in and brought us back to the point of the meeting, reminding the police that a year was coming up since Rae had made her initial report to police. "Can you please tell us where things are and what to expect next?" she said.

At that point, Officer Snair dropped a bombshell. She said that the police had conflicting evidence. This was the first time Leah, Rae, and I had heard this, and we all fell quiet. "What conflicting evidence?" Rae eventually asked. When Officer Snair told us that she couldn't divulge any more, since the investigation was ongoing, Rae stood up, pounded her fists on the table and kicked back her chair. "What conflicting evidence?!" she shouted.

Officer Snair repeated she could not say.

"Why is everything I put my faith in a joke?" Rae yelled as she stormed out of the room.

At the front desk, Rae stopped. She thrust her phone up toward the face of the duty sergeant and asked him to read the messages Blake had been sending her, messages saying she was a slut and worthless. "Are you going to do anything about this? What does it take for you people to actually get off your chairs and do work?" she screamed.

Leah and I came running up behind her. The duty sergeant was staring at us with bug eyes, bewildered by what was happening, as

Leah and I pulled Rae from the police station. "Peanut," I said when we were in the car, her face still crimson and sweaty, "let's get away from here."

When I was a child, my father would take me fishing. We would head out into the Bay of Quinte near Trenton, Ontario, in an old aluminum boat — the motor so temperamental we were never sure whether we would be rowing or motoring back to shore — and sit for hours as the steam of dawn evaporated. I would catch bass and perch — once, a three-foot-long eel. I'd look over at my father, bright-eyed, searching for his approval and his praise. He would stare at the fish as it flopped on the bottom of the boat, shake his head, and watch as I withdrew the hook to toss the tiny thing back into the water. It was unsaid between us, but the fish were too small. I needed to catch something bigger.

My father was the son of his own quiet, distant dad, overworked at the mill, pressured to support a family in the sputtering Nova Scotia economy of the 1930s and '40s. His mother was passive, afraid of her husband, only alive when alone in the house or picking blueberries with me and her other grandchildren. She was different then, it seemed — chatty, confident — but around my grandfather she disappeared, much like my own mother around her husband. My father had become his father, absorbed with work and providing for his family, yet distant from that same family. My brother Jim became a star footballer, but Dad never attended any of the games. At my high-school graduation it was just my mother, younger brothers, and my sister cheering me on.

In one of my last visits to Ottawa before Dad's death in 2006, he took me into the kitchen. It was just him and me, my mother asleep. My father was flagging then, his mind slow, his eyes watery and dazed a lot of the time, his speech awkward, like he was waiting for his mind to parcel out the words.

He poured us each a Scotch and had me sit across from him. Then he said nothing for the longest time.

I watched some flies hovering over a bowl of fruit.

"I wasn't a very good father," he finally murmured. His voice was liquidy, his eyes bloodshot, like he was about to cry. Then he shook his head, stood up, and went to bed. I believed he was trying to say both that he was sorry and that he did the best with what he had.

As Rae and I drove home from the police station that August day, I thought of Dad. And I remembered the summer Rae was eight. I had taken her to Canadian Tire where we bought fishing rods — hers a kid-sized pole — and fishing licenses. Then Rae and I went out to Lake Micmac in Dartmouth. We parked ourselves in a secluded area on some rocks and fished. Rae pulled in the first catch of the day, a rock bass. She struggled hard with the tiny pole, refusing my help, and eventually managing to bring in the jumpy little fella. She squealed as the fish flapped around her feet until I caught hold of it. I taught Rae then that we didn't need to keep it, eat it, or kill it. I slipped the fish hook out of the rock bass's mouth and threw it back into the lake. After, I told her how proud of her I was. Catching fish wasn't our purpose; our purpose was being together.

On that ride home, I suggested that maybe Rae would want to take a holiday, get away — my brother Jim and his wife, Shari, owned a beautiful cottage in Ontario, north of Peterborough. I suggested Rae might spend the summer there.

"You can go fishing, be out in nature, maybe see some deer or a black bear," I said. "Your cousins will be there, Julia and Ty."

Her face was still tear-stained and red from her fury at the police station, but she forced a smile and nodded. She too knew it was time to do something drastic, even if that meant we would be separated. She needed a fresh beginning.

For most of August, Rae stayed at Jim's cottage. It was exactly what she needed: a completely new environment. Rae played board games — Yahtzee, Trivial Pursuit, Monopoly — with her cousins Julia, who was seventeen, and Ty, fifteen. She learned how to jet-ski and wakeboard. She cut herself off from technology, except to call Leah or me with updates. She would chirp into the phone about all she was doing: fishing, bonfires at night, staring at the starry sky, long walks on the dirt roads. Rae whispered in one conversation a few weeks into her stay that she hadn't cut since the day after her arrival. She wasn't doing drugs, and she was sleeping too, deep sleeps, with dreams. "I'm even seeing crows in my dreams, Dad. Crows, like they are trying to tell me they're watching over me." Leah had brought up Rae and her sisters to respect the idea of spirit animals: the belief that every person has a particular animal species watching over them, sometimes for their entire lives, other times for the course of a conflict or life transition.

Rae and Shari developed a special bond that summer, after the two found they shared a love of midnight skinny-dipping in the lake. One morning, Rae sat on the deck of the cottage and looked out over the lake, her eyes trailing a family of loons. A mist was rising and the sun's morning rays stretched through the pine and fir trees on the opposite shore, dancing on the still water like the flames of tea lights. Shari watched for a bit and marvelled at Rae's serenity in nature. Then she slipped down beside Rae and listened patiently as Rae told her everything that had happened since November 12, 2011.

Shari, Rae said, reminded her of Renee. She was compassionate, youthful, a friend as well as a mother to her children. She often took in her kids' friends when they needed a place to stay. Like with Chloe at Prince Andrew High School, Rae did little without Shari by her side. She told Shari that being at the cottage was the first time in a long time she felt alive. Swimming helped her connect with her body again; being in the water, she could feel the work of her skin, bones, and muscles to move, strengthen, and nurture her.

After the cottage, Rae and Jim's family returned to Ottawa. "I belong here," Rae wrote, after texting me photographs of her and her cousin Julia at the Canadian Museum of History, dressed in colonial women's outfits — long cotton dresses and wide-brimmed hats. "I want to stay here."

I too wanted Rae to stay and live with Jim and Shari and her cousins, who made her feel like she belonged again in a world with teenagers. After months of not finding an adult to connect with, Leah and I felt relieved Rae had found someone like Shari to trust with her feelings. I even went so far as to think that if Rae did remain in Ottawa, I would move there part-time too. Rae would live at Shari and Jim's house, turning the guest bedroom overlooking the pool into her own room. Rae wrote up a list of all the clothes, books, and supplies she needed and sent it to Leah.

Then, Rae changed her mind. A couple days before school was to start, she said she was watching how close Julia and Ty were to each other. Rae wanted that closeness with her own sisters Teaghan, who was then four, and Temyson, who was eight. Rae missed them. She was coming home.

I expressed concern, but Rae consoled me by telling me that after the summer, after spending time with kids her age who accepted her, she felt she could navigate high school again. She wanted to attend Citadel High, in my catchment area, and live with Krista and me during the week, and with her sisters and Leah on the weekends. Inspired by Julia, who was a good student like her, Rae began to make a checklist of the things she wanted to accomplish before graduation. The list was different than the one she had written at the start of high school. It didn't include a social life, dances, prom, and joining the cheerleading squad. She still wanted a boyfriend and to be on the honour roll, but her main goal was to be left alone. To be, she wrote, invisible.

In September 2012, Rae started grade 11 at Citadel High School, a newly built school in a sprawling, modern, glass-walled building. Even on cloudy days, the halls were bright and cheerful.

For a few days, it seemed Citadel would be good for her. Rae was taking math and science courses in the International Baccalaureate program. She was also picking up a required French course. At nights, she was focused on her homework and moving ahead in class.

Then, on the third day, the whispers started. As she walked down the hallway, Rae was certain kids were talking about her. They would look up at her and smirk and then quickly dart their eyes away. At first she thought she was just being paranoid.

On the last day of the first full week of school, on her way to last period, a guy strolled up to her and thrust his phone into Rae's face. She stared at the photo. The photo of her, taken on that night.

"I know that's you," the boy said with a laugh.

He left her there, the words *slut* and *whore* ringing again in her ears. For the rest of that week she lay in bed, unable to do much except go to the washroom and eat a few spoonfuls of soup. She started cutting again, cutting deep, after having spent the summer clean. I bandaged her up and washed her bedding. I held her in my arms and rocked her to sleep.

She quit school. "The kids are saying shit about me," she told me. No matter how far she went, she said, those girls would find her and the picture would stalk her. I suggested she move to Ottawa after all. She said no. She asked me if it would be okay for her to get her high-school degree online instead. She was a bright student, and I knew she would study hard. I agreed she could try, but Ottawa would be left on the table if things didn't work out.

Chapter Eleven

Throughout the fall of 2012, Leah called the police for updates and demanded to be told more about the conflicting evidence. For nearly two months, she and Detective Constable Snair played phone tag.

Rae began her home schooling and got part-time jobs babysitting and working at a grocery store to keep her busy. She wasn't happy, but she was working hard with her schooling and she seemed to enjoy it. Her anxiety seemed to be far lower, and I was optimistic that slowly we were getting somewhere.

Then, on October 31, Sergeant Legere connected with Leah. He reported that, following a meeting with the Crown attorney, the police had decided that there was not enough evidence to proceed with sexual assault charges. However, the police were still looking into child-pornography charges. On November 14, Sergeant Legere told Leah that child-pornography charges were not going to be laid either.

On that phone call, Leah asked Sergeant Legere to tell Rae directly. "You at least owe her that," she said.

Immediately after Rae spoke to Sergeant Legere, she texted me:

> I hate the police.

But then she said she had another plan.

> I am going to the media and I want you and my mother behind me.

That night, Rae laid out her research — as if she had prepared for the police closing her file all along. She had a list of reporters, some of whom I'd worked with as both a photographer and cameraman. (Leah had in fact gone to the media, earlier in the year, contacting a local talk radio program. But at that time, the case was still open and the host felt having Rae on air discussing her experiences might hinder the police investigation.)

Rae talked to me then about another girl with a similar story. Amanda Todd, a fifteen-year-old in British Columbia, had hung herself nearly a month earlier, on October 10, 2012, after years of being bullied, beaten, and slut-shamed. Amanda's ordeal started when she was in grade 7. A cyberpredator in Europe lured her into revealing her breasts online while she was taking part in what she thought was a singing program. When Amanda refused to show her body to the man a second time, he sent the photographs of her breasts to all of her social-media contacts and went on to set up a fake Amanda Todd Facebook account, the profile picture an image of her naked torso.

Instead of the wider community being shocked and stunned, demanding that the RCMP shut the Facebook page down, neighbours started to shun Amanda and her family. Like Rae, Amanda was harassed out of one school, and then another. Boys used her, girls beat her up. Like Rae, Amanda had nowhere to turn, nowhere to hide.

Rae had learned about the story after Amanda posted a YouTube video chronicling the bullying, stalking, girl-on-girl fighting, depression, anxiety, and cutting she was enduring on a series of flashcards. Rae talked to me about how she wished she had known about Amanda earlier, reached out, and had the foresight to suggest they fight for justice together. "I can at least use the media now to tell them who I am, tell them Amanda's story, and make people understand," Rae said.

I was receptive to Rae's idea, but at the same time terrified. Rae was so angry with the police, and so physically vulnerable to self-harm if the reception to her story was anything but positive. If she was going to do something like this, I wanted her to be emotionally strong first. I knew well enough, from my days as a journalist, that sexual assault survivors, unlike the victims of any other crime, are often dragged through the mud, with every aspect of their story picked apart, chewed, and then spat out. The hateful messages our family had received, the vitriol directed toward Rae and the rest of us, made that seem even more likely. I wanted to shield her from more torment and abuse from the community until she was ready to navigate such a storm. Rae had spent the past year being threatened, taunted, and disbelieved. She would even learn about — and see for herself — graffiti about her scrawled in the stalls of public bathrooms in Cole Harbour, and in the schools she attended.

But Rae was becoming a crusader — maybe this, if nothing else, was a way to turn her despair into something good. She said she wanted to go to university and study law. First, get a bachelor's degree at Mount Saint Vincent University in Halifax, known for its feminist campus culture, and then a law degree at the larger Dalhousie University. She wanted to defend teen survivors of rape.

Leah and I encouraged Rae to give the idea of going to the media some time, so we could all prepare for any blowback to come.

On November 12, 2012, Rae posted several messages on Twitter. One read: "Almost a year has passed and I still cry sometimes."

Rae returned to the SPCA as a volunteer to walk dogs. She spent time with her sisters, throwing a baseball around with Temyson (who later represented Canada in softball at the Pan Am Games, as a pitcher). She built enormous doll mansions with Teaghan, for her toys and miniature animals.

She also met Chris, a new boyfriend, near Christmas. They met through Chloe, with whom Rae had been back in touch. Chris was paying his own way through college, studying to be a pipe fitter, working nearly full time as an apprentice. When I met him, he shook my hand and looked me in the eye. I could see the way he looked at Rae, with real love, and I was happy for that. Not wanting a repeat of what happened with Blake, Rae told Chris as much of her story as she could before they started dating. She wanted him to hear her side of things before he heard it from someone else. She gave him the option to not pursue the relationship, but to break it off then. He didn't, and they quickly grew close.

Rae closed the door on her former life as best she could — including any dreams she had that the boys would be punished. She moved back in with Leah to help care for her sisters and be close to them and went back to Prince Andrew High, where she still had friends.

Krista and I celebrated Rae's seventeenth birthday by enrolling her in a driving course. We had dinner at Zen Cuisine and Rae had her favourite, lemon chicken.

That winter of 2013, for the first time in more than a year, it felt like we were steadily, with no dead ends or zigzagging back and forth, getting our Rae back. She was moody and still bitter and hated the police. She would feel temporarily stunned on the rare occasion that she saw someone from Cole Harbour High at the mall, or when she was out with Chris. The chest contractions would happen; the panic would move through her. But just as quickly as the anxiety came, Rae would use the self-care techniques she'd learned to talk herself off the proverbial ledge. She seemed to be healing.

In the evening of April 2, 2013, I parked my car on Quinpool Road, in front of the West End Baptist Church, and looked around. Halifax was in the transition from winter to spring. Night fell later, but the branches of the trees were still naked. The air was dewy. The night sky was clear. The stars overhead shone bright.

Rae was inside the church, in a one-on-one counselling session with a new therapist. I was nervous, always holding out hope that one of these days Rae would meet another Renee.

To distract myself, I had turned my attention to setting up my newest toy, an attachable dashboard camera, when Rae came bouncing out the church's front door, her long legs — Rae was now five foot eleven — taking great strides toward me, her dark brown hair now dyed auburn, worn loose and wavy, flying up behind her like the train of a veil. Her jacket and hoodie were open. Underneath she was wearing a white T-shirt. She was smiling. I relaxed.

"Dad, I booked another session," she said. She beamed as she hopped into the passenger seat.

"Great," I said, trying to hide my surprise and, well, relief. Rae now entered relationships, from friends to teachers to counsellors, expecting to be betrayed, so the fact that she had booked a follow-up meeting meant that there was something positive there.

"Can we go to McDonald's?" she asked as I pulled away from the whitewashed church, pointing the Fiat toward Highway 111.

"It's late," I said. "You shouldn't eat at this hour."

She started to whimper, pouted a bit, and fell quiet. Eventually she said, "Dad, can you believe my meeting was in a church? Look at the irony. *God hasn't helped me.*"

I swallowed hard and kept my eyes on the road. I didn't know what to say; since everything happened to Rae, I had found myself tongue-tied a lot, walking on eggshells, not wanting to make things worse. Rae leaned toward me, swinging the palm of her hand in front of my face. "Dad, are you listening?" she said. "Did you hear what I said? God hasn't helped me."

"What happened to you is not God," I whispered, trying to think of what Reverend Ron would say.

Rae's phone croaked then, her ringtone set to the sound of a bullfrog. She leaned back in her seat and I could hear Chris's voice on the other end, even though Rae cupped her hand over the phone and turned her head away from me. "I love you," I heard him say.

"I love you, too," Rae said in a barely audible voice.

"Rae, I've never heard you say you love anyone other than family before. Do you really love Chris?" I asked after she hung up. I hoped she did. I wanted that for her.

"I think so," she mused. She said she felt Chris didn't judge her. As much as she could love someone, she said, she thought she did Chris. Rae reached up and turned off my dashboard camera, which had been recording what would turn out to be our last conversation.

Rae suddenly became fiery, accusing her friend Mandy — who was having troubles with her mother and living with Leah and Rae temporarily — of breaking her iPad.

I pulled over onto the shoulder of the highway and examined the iPad. It was my old one, which I had given to Rae when I upgraded to a newer model. "I don't think Mandy did anything," I said after a few minutes. "It looks fine. Are you sure she's not joking with you?"

"People are not supposed to touch other people's stuff. People can't just take what they want," she said. I reached over and rubbed Rae's shoulder. She squirmed as if to pull away, then stopped. Rae's trigger, one of the main trauma triggers that sent her head spinning, was any hint, any whiff, that something was being taken away from her or from someone else. This triggered Rae, dark and unreachable, scared me. "God's abandoned me," she said, turning her head away. "The Devil has done more for me."

As I started driving again, we bantered back and forth: me trying to buoy Rae back to the surface, Rae seeming to drift further into a stormy sea.

I pulled up in front of Leah's house. I spied Rae's blue hammock, which she must have just pulled out of winter storage and set up. The hammock was swaying in the breeze. The light from the streetlamps cast long, dancing shadows over it and my car. I leaned over and kissed Rae on the cheek.

"I love you," I said.

She gathered up her purse, stuffing the iPad back inside.

Rae reached for the handle and then stopped. She turned slowly back and looked at me. Her gaze was deep and penetrating but her face vacant, like her eyes wanted to tell me something that her mind hadn't caught up to yet. "I love you too, Dad," she eventually said. "I love you too."

Chapter Twelve

Rae had been ditching classes again, showing up at school and then disappearing. The guidance counsellor had suggested that she consider taking a break from school, instead studying online and working on finding a job.

I imagine that April 4 started off like any other day. Leah would drag Rae out of bed at about 8 a.m. Rae would fumble her way to the kitchen and watch while Teaghan ate breakfast; Temyson was too busy changing outfits and messaging her friends to join them. Mandy, living with Rae and Leah, maybe meandered in, grabbed an apple and a slice of toast, and said she would walk with Temyson to school.

Leah would have stuffed a yogurt cup and some nuts into her purse and headed out with her partner, Jason, who had moved in a few months earlier. Jason would have dropped Leah at work, and Teaghan at her dad's, on the way to his own job as a city bus driver.

When the house was quiet, except for the panting of the SPCA dogs that Leah was caring for, Rae, I do know, planned her day, starting with arranging for her and Chris to drop off her resumé off at various places.

At about 11:30 a.m., Rae took the rescue dogs in the house to the parkette down the road. There was a poodle named Frankie, a large rottweiler named George, and that gentle German shepherd with the giant puppy feet, now an adult, who had been bounced from one home to the next before being deposited back at Leah's house.

After Chris and Rae had driven around for most of the afternoon, they got together with some of Chris's friends. Another boy made a comment about Rae. A negative comment.

That's when it started.

Rae felt Chris didn't stand up to him; stand up for her.

The panic started to bubble.

Rae arrived home at 10:30 p.m., her anxiety now having moved into full-blown terror.

At some point, she texted her aunt Shari:

> I don't feel loved. I feel all alone. I am angry.

Shari messaged back:

> You are more than loved. You are an angel in this world.

Rae was sliding backwards: the strange bedroom, the stink of boys, the stares, the glares, the graffiti on the bathroom walls, the social-media messages, the girls harassing her from school to school to school.

Chris and Rae connected. Chris tried to reason, tried to reassure Rae that he loved her, that he was sorry. But by then, Rae was no longer in control. She wasn't listening to kind words, just the words she had been told over the past year.

> Slut

> Whore

> She wanted it

> She's good for one thing and one thing only

She hung up on Chris and then threw her phone across the room. She moved to the bathroom.

After a while, Mandy knocked on the bathroom door, wanting in, wanting to know if Rae was okay. When she heard nothing, Mandy called for Leah.

No one expected the worst, just that Rae was upset, perhaps brooding in the bathtub, listening to music on her headphones.

With no sound coming from inside the bathroom, coming from Rae, Leah finally broke down the door.

Rae was unconscious, lying on the floor.

She'd taken her glasses off, and placed them carefully on the counter by the sink.

Chapter Thirteen

When I first joined the navy, I had a diver friend, a young guy named Stéphan. He was French Canadian and spoke English with a thick rural Québécois accent. A good guy, a solid guy, maybe twenty-five at most. He had a pretty wife named Linda and a bouncing baby boy that looked just like him. Stéphan, Linda, and I would go to house parties together, and Stéphan and I always ended the nights with a game of beer caps, though we were usually too tipsy to keep track of who was actually winning.

One Thursday afternoon in early November 1988, Stéphan was doing a bottom search as part of a mine-training exercise near McNabs Island in Halifax Harbour. In a bottom search, we would set up search grids on the floor of the sea and prowl the area looking for mines. The exercise was to prepare us for situations where we'd have to find live mines. When Stéphan and his diving buddy surfaced from the mission, the guys in the Zodiac boat pulled the other guy in first. When they turned to get Stéphan, he was gone — he had slipped back under the surface.

A diving team, including me, searched the murky bottom of Halifax Harbour. On that particular afternoon, the silence under the sea was dense, almost suffocating — not the gentle, otherworldly hum that I usually found so calming.

The official autopsy reported that Stéphan's rebreather hadn't been hooked up right. In an operating rebreather, as divers exhale into the canister, soda lime scrubs the carbon dioxide out of the breath, so when the person inhales, it's pure oxygen. We do exercises as naval divers to prepare us for such situations. Stéphan was instead breathing in his own exhaled breath, and the CO_2 was building up rapidly in his blood.

I found Stéphan. It was late the following afternoon; he'd been down at the bottom of the harbour alone for more than twenty-four hours. He looked alive, drifting with the current, except for his eyes, which were closed like he was sleeping. His hands were up, as if reaching for me, or waving at me. His dark hair drifted out of the hood of his wetsuit, danced in the water, and brushed his face.

My first instinct was to swim in the opposite direction, to get away — I guess to pretend I hadn't found him, that somewhere he was still alive.

In the Zodiac, bringing Stéphan's body to shore, I cried. With a crisp autumn wind slapping at my cheeks and bouncing off my wetsuit, the sunset casting an orange-red hue in the western sky, the eastern sky already indigo, I wept like a baby. The beauty around me — the curved coast of fir trees, maples in fall golds and reds, and the sound of water lapping against the side of the boat, were at odds with the deep pain I felt. I thought then how spectacular and fragile life was.

When I sat with Stéphan's wife, Linda, the evening after I found him, flipping through Polaroids of this loving and young family that should have had more years together, I thought how quickly people's lives can change — like passing out, a snap of the fingers. What holds us together are those moments in between, as Reverend Ron would say, when we have surrendered to God and to the beauty inside and all around us.

I groaned. Five a.m. April 5. Krista set her alarm to this time every day. Truncated, ear-splitting beeps — like the alarms on naval ships announcing emergencies or drills — dug their way into my sleep.

Every morning, Krista woke up at this time to work out on the treadmill. Krista, my anchor, who can put her hand on my shoulder and steady me in the midst of my stormy seas.

For the past few weeks, since Rae seemed to be steady and walking on both feet, I had put my phone on Do Not Disturb mode at night to try and get back sleep that I had lost since *before*. I was taking this reprieve for me, to settle myself, so I could be rested.

I heard Krista start up the treadmill. I smelled coffee percolating.

I moaned and pulled Krista's pillow over my eyes, hoping to catch another hour and a half of sleep. But Ozzie nudged me with his nose.

"You want to go for a pee, buddy?" I asked, dragging myself up. I looked over at him. Usually, when he saw me coming, he would start hopping from foot to foot and a grin would spread from ear to ear, making him look a little like the Joker in the Batman comic books. This time, though, Ozzie planted his legs and whined.

"What is it?" I asked him. He tilted his head and stared at me.

I stood up, pulling on my housecoat as if to go downstairs to let him outside, but his legs were still. His eyes were glossy, yearning, like Rae's eyes the night before, trying to tell me something.

"Buddy?"

Dread moved through me then. Some knowing. I instinctively looked over at my phone. The light indicating I had a message was flashing. I quickly flipped through my call history. Starting at 11:30 the night before, calls began flooding in, one after the other, from Leah, some just minutes apart.

I quickly punched in the password to access my voicemail. Messages. Several of them. *All Leah.* Calm and collected.

"Glen, Rae hanged herself last night."

"Glen, Rae hanged herself last night."

"Glen, Rae hanged herself last night."

I wiped my perspiring forehead with a shaky hand, thinking, because of the flatness in Leah's voice, that I must have heard wrong. *I am tired*, I told myself. *I am trapped in my nightmares.*

I replayed the messages again.

And again.

Until it sunk in: I was awake. And the phone was ringing.

"Glen," Leah said when I picked up. "Rae hanged herself last night. We're at the hospital. I need you to get to the hospital right away. The doctors are not detecting any brain activity..."

My fingertips dug into the walls, my legs straining to hold up my body, which was dead weight, as I walked toward Krista.

When I saw Krista, I opened my mouth but no words came out.

I flicked the overhead light switch off and on to get her attention. Krista stopped running. The machine came to a slow stall.

She hopped off and moved toward me.

She knew before I told her.

Krista and I were buzzed into the intensive care unit at the Halifax Infirmary.

A doctor — fit, with sandy blonde hair, wearing a white lab coat overtop green surgical scrubs — moved toward us. When he drew close, he splayed his hands out in front of him. "Stop," he ordered us. "Who are you?" Even his voice was youthful.

"I'm Rae...Rehtaeh's Parsons's dad," I stammered. My eyes and throat were swollen. Tears sat pooling, like a gully during spring thaw.

The doctor said nothing and, for a moment, I wondered if I had even said the words.

"What do you know?" he finally asked, his body barring our way into the ward. I peered over his shoulder, trying to see what he was blocking. Nothing but a long, white corridor. I turned back to him. He looked like an outdoors guide — someone who should be giving me directions on a hike, not telling me my daughter was about to die. "What do you know?" he repeated, and this time his voice was strong, serious, and deep. He was transforming into a doctor.

"She doesn't have a lot of brain activity," I croaked out.

"Okay, I just needed you to know, before you go in there: it looks really grim."

I gripped Krista's hand so tight that when I looked down, her knuckles had turned white.

I released some of the pressure and we followed the doctor.

With each step I berated myself.

Last night, before I turned my phone off, I had thought of calling Rae. Three times, the thought had popped into my head.

Three times.

Why had I not called? Why hadn't I listened?

Kids are not supposed to die before their parents. That thought sent pain right through my body, sharp, piercing pain, like a sword was cutting me into two.

I couldn't look, not where I was supposed to.

Leah. My eyes, like lasers, went to her first, sitting on a metal chair to the right of the hospital bed.

She looked up, her eyes bloodshot, her skin talcum-powder white. Her chin-length blonde hair looked brittle, like her.

She motioned with her head to look at Rae, not at her.

Rae's bed was in the centre of the dimly lit room. Leah had covered her in the leopard blanket from Rae's bedroom. Rae was hooked up to a heart-monitoring machine.

She looks too warm. Too comfortable. Too cozy.

Her glasses were off, sitting on a side table. I reached for them, to put them back on her face.

You never take these off, I said in my head. *You're going to wake up soon.*

The heart monitor showed beats, slow but steady. My own heart fluttered and, for a moment, I thought the doctor was wrong. Rae would survive this.

I leaned over and kissed my baby girl on the forehead. I then moved my lips up close to her left ear. "When you wake up, I will take you to McDonald's," I whispered.

I smoothed out her hair that smelled of scented shampoo — lemongrass maybe and a hint of lavender.

"The doctors will give us a briefing to talk about what is going on," Leah said in that same voice from the telephone — too steady, but now also muffled, like she was talking to me from behind a wall.

A scream began to build inside me. "What . . . what . . . what happened?" I tried to ask, but I couldn't push the words out in order. Rae had been doing so well.

I heard Rae's voice from two nights earlier:

"God's abandoned me."

"The Devil has done more for me."

"The hospital can't certify her death until there is no more brain activity," Leah continued, her voice buzzing softly, like a blackfly in summer zooming close to my ear. I wanted to swat it away. "The hospital can't issue a death certificate because Rae's still technically alive. But she doesn't have enough brain activity to function. Soon, she'll shut down. We have to wait."

Wait for my daughter to die.

It was like the room moved away and only Rae remained. I leaned in close again and started talking, mumbling, rambling.

"I should have done more for you. I should have fought. I should have told you you were not alone. I should have stood up for you. I should have stood up for me. Rae, can you ever ever forgive me?"

Krista reached for me. She touched my arm. She told me I wasn't making sense. But I was, I charged back. I was finally telling Rae the truth.

Blinded by a darkness that I couldn't keep hidden any longer, I dashed out of the room. I felt my way down the hallway, my sweaty palms staining the white walls as I pushed myself forward.

I slammed my way into a staff bathroom and bolted the door.

I gripped the sink and stared into the mirror.

The person looking back was me, but as a seven-year-old boy, hiding in the tall, yellowed grass of the prairies, my first 35 mm camera in one hand and balled earth in the other.

I heard my heavy breathing.

I heard footsteps.

And then calm.

I looked up at clouds. Floating like ships.

I just had to be still, to be quiet, to be unseen, and it would all pass over. *The danger would pass.*

A wail then came out of me like no sound I had ever made before. Krista later told me it sounded inhuman.

Now, in that mirror, staring back at me, was my father's shocked face. I saw his back, straight and proud, his broad shoulders rounded, as he turned away and walked back up a set of stairs.

I pounded my fist against the wall with such force my knuckles started to bleed.

"I made a deal that I would not be you, Dad," I yelled. "I wouldn't turn my back on my child."

I yanked the paper-towel dispenser off the wall and threw it on the floor.

I kicked it.

I kicked the wall.

I heard voices outside shouting, asking if I was all right.

Krista's voice was one of them.

My knees could no longer hold me up. I sank to the ground.

I was sitting not far from Rae's room in the ICU, in the hallway, on a chair or a couch, I don't remember. It could have been the waiting room or right in front of the triage desk. Wherever it was, I was numb, not really there, drifting with Rae and my memories.

Leah and I couldn't be in the same room at the same time. Something was just unsaid between us, at least on that first day with

Rae in the hospital. Maybe it was because when we were together we were confronted with the truth: our child was about to die. But in our separation we could tell ourselves a different story: that Rae would wake up, that this crisis would end, that we would have another chance to heal our daughter. I knew for a fact that Rae hadn't done this to hurt us — Leah, me, Krista, her little sisters whom she loved with every breath. Rae was trying to escape. What she did was impulsive, desperate, an attempt to stifle the pain inside. Like when she would dig the razor deep into her arms. She had to resort to something drastic to forget.

She wasn't like this, not at all, before that day, I remembered Leah saying to someone, maybe a nurse, when asked about Rae's psychiatric history.

Every so often, I could hear a doctor stopping to talk to me, to reiterate that Rae had very little brain activity and, as a result, her organs were slowly shutting down. It was merely a matter of time, hours or days, maybe weeks. I heard myself and Leah, briefly brought together, maybe late in the afternoon, in an office on the ICU floor, telling a hospital administrator that Rae would have wanted her organs donated. Rae was always about helping others.

"Thinking of others, wanting to give back," I mumbled. I know I signed some papers authorizing the donations. I recall hearing someone say they already had matches for her kidneys and her heart.

The nurses monitored Rae's blood pressure, kept her warm, stabilized her, and changed her catheter. Rae was in a single room in the ICU, her bed in the middle of the room with chairs placed on both sides of it, the headrest set against a wall. Her room had a large window that overlooked the Nova Scotia Museum of Natural History.

When it was my turn to be with Rae, when Leah would leave to grab a coffee or talk to the doctors, I would sit beside her, holding her warm hand, listening to the beeping and whirring of the machines, and staring out that window at the museum, a boxy, three-storey 1970s structure. When she was a child I brought her there often. She loved the bee exhibit and the history of the First Nations, the Mi'kmaq, who lived here on these lands long before us, and the dinosaurs that lived here long before them. Her forehead would furrow and her eyes would narrow, like I was privy to her absorbing and processing everything she was learning about the world and our history. One summer when Rae and I went to the museum, the staff had curated a live butterfly display, and the tiny creatures would hover around Rae, then settle on her shoulders and in the palms of her hands.

Krista called my boss, Ken, at the Apple Store, to tell him I wouldn't be coming in for a while and why. She also got in touch with my family, and she let me know that my sister and mother were on their way.

When twilight set in on that Friday, and the lights of the ICU seemed to brighten, I walked out of Rae's room to find my little brother, Casey, waiting for me. He'd taken the first flight he could get out of Ottawa, and he looked surprisingly neat and trim. We took seats side by side in the waiting room, and Casey was quiet and still, like when we were small kids and would play the card game War — which, despite the name, we played civilly and quietly. It was like he knew that his presence alone was all I needed. I wondered if I had been wrong all along about him, and he was the brave one of the family: exploring our darkness to guide us all.

Chris, Rae's boyfriend, came in late on that Friday too, after Casey left to get settled in a hotel nearby. Sitting down, Chris put his face into the palms of his hands and wept. I bent down in front of him and slowly pried his hands away. "Do not think you are to blame for this," I whispered to him. Mandy had told me about the fight he and Rae had had.

For months, Chris had been Rae's safe harbour, and I was grateful for that, I told him. But I knew, no matter what I said, he would consider what Rae did his fault. A shiver ran through me as I thought how, for the rest of his life, he would be carrying the burden of guilt, though it unquestionably belonged elsewhere.

In the hospital with Rae, I found myself slipping slowly backwards in time. Rae was getting younger in my mind: she was running in and out of the waves on our walks by the sea, picking up sea-worn stones and laughing.

I had heard stories about how, when a loved one dies, you can feel them. I'd had such an experience back in 2006. I woke up in the middle of the night with goosebumps on the back of my neck, certain that there was someone else in the bed with me. For a moment I froze, then I ran through my military combat training, planning how to fight off this intruder. It was like he or she had crawled under the covers beside me, nestled in close, rubbing my head. My cellphone rang, startling me. I leapt out of bed quickly, jumping with fists up, only to find no one there. On the other end of the phone was my sister, Kim. Dad had died.

I didn't feel Rae, not like I had my dad that night. But I thought I could hear her when I was returning from the cafeteria with coffee. I'd round a corner and could swear she was calling out to me. Dozing in the armchair in the waiting room, I heard her voice, as a seven-year-old, saying "Daddy." For months after Stéphan's passing, he haunted my dreams. I would see him floating at the bottom of the sea, reaching for me, and hear his voice calling for help. It was like he was trying to tell me something. I could swear Rae was trying to contact me too.

Before I went home that Friday night to get a few hours' sleep, shower, and change, I went to Rae's ICU room. It must have been close to midnight. The overhead lights were dimmed, and the lights from the Museum of Natural History floated into the room through the window, like stardust. I broke down, buried my head in the crook of Rae's neck, soaking her sheets, her hair, and her cozy leopard-print blanket.

"Please tell me how you want me to help you," I whimpered, my heart bleeding, seeping blood and grief like another blanket on top of Rae. "Please give me a message. What do you want me to do? I love you so much."

Chapter Fourteen

Sometime late in the evening on Friday, April 5, 2013, Leah went home to shower and change, and to check in on Teaghan and Temyson, who were being watched by Marianne.

Of course, sleep eluded both of us. Nights, I would soon discover, were the hardest. That's when, lying dormant, unable to sleep, my thoughts would spin. I would second- and triple-guess all of my actions and wonder what I could have done differently. I would run through the mistakes I felt I had made and berate myself: *If I had done this, that way, Rae would still be alive.* When the shame and remorse became too painful to sit in, I would play head games with myself and pretend that Rae was really alive, as if I was just stuck in a bad dream. Or I would bargain with God, asking to be taken instead. I remembered a trip I had once taken to Santorini, an island in Greece with hundreds upon hundreds of churches. I asked a local why so many shrines and small chapels had been built there, and he explained that every time a fisherman got stuck in a storm at sea, he would pray to God that, if he made it back ashore safely, he would build a church. "I'll build you a church," I cried out one night. "God, just bring her back."

People deal with the death of a child in different ways. I dealt with it in the worst way: I shut down. I closed myself off from everyone else, not so much because I wanted to, but because I didn't know how such grief could possibly be endured. I had moments when I wondered if I was even alive — maybe I was dying, not Rae, and everything I thought I was experiencing was just a mirage.

Leah, on the other hand, needed to reach out, to be held, to share. That's how she believed society should function, she once told me: people should carry each other's burdens and celebrate each other's victories. "It's where we're headed," she had told me once when we were together, "where we have to go, because everyone wakes up at some point and realizes they're alone and frightened and they've been living their lives all wrong."

Part of her way of connecting to others was posting updates on Rae's condition on Facebook, expressing her anguish:

> My beautiful girl struggles with each breath . . . she fought depression for over a year now . . . She found herself in a web of betrayal where friends turned against her, still she tried to get up over and over again. She was running on fumes and still she tried . . . they walked the streets happy. She sits in ICU fighting to survive. That's the world we live in!

The post was supposed to be a message to Leah's friends and family. She never intended her words to go beyond those few who had stood beside her since November 12, 2011. But its impact soon spread beyond our circles, beyond our city, beyond even our country. We couldn't have known then that it would become the call to action that it did; that the impact of that one message would reverberate so powerfully.

Early on April 6, some of Rae's friends came to the hospital after seeing Leah's message. Chloe and Mandy had made Rae feel like a normal teenage girl, not a pariah or victim or perpetrator or harlot. They had taken her to movies and indulged in coffee-shop gossip, sneaking out to parks and into the pedestrian tunnels that run underneath Cole Harbour's Forest Hills Parkway to experiment with weed.

They sat by Rae's bed, held her hand, and stroked her forehead. Rae had told me once that eyes tell a person's story. Some eyes draw a person in, other eyes deflect, and still others are like a slate, revealing nothing. These were the eyes, she had said, that scared her the most. These were the eyes of the boys in the hallways at school. Chloe and Mandy cried and their eyes gave them away — they cared, and they loved her.

Childhood friends came after Mandy and Chloe left. Emily and her sister Lindsay, a year apart but to me twins, who in their contradictions formed a whole. I smiled when I saw them, remembering their sleepovers with Rae. Emily couldn't spend a night apart from her family when she was young. I could time it: by 9:00 she'd have a stomach ache, and by 9:30 she'd be whimpering to go home. But when Lindsay joined her, it was like our home became Emily's, and Emily would stay right through the night, flopping into the kitchen in the morning in her oversized Disney character slippers for a breakfast of pancakes topped with maple syrup and gummy bears. When the sisters would arrive for their sleepovers, they'd head right to Rae's bedroom to haul out her animal collection: Hammy the hamster, hermit crabs, a mouse named Snoop, and a gecko named Soup. The hermit crabs would pinch Rae's hand with their razor-sharp claws, not wanting the attention of these cooing girls pretending they were dolls, rocking them and singing lullabies and songs from movies.

About midday on Saturday the people who had said "this isn't our problem" started to show up. The kids who weren't there for Rae, who had disappeared and remained silent. The bystanders. The boys and girls she went to prom with in middle school. Those girls who, in our languid summers, would dress up like the Spice Girls and put on performances in the front yard of Leah's house. (Rae was always Sporty Spice, strong and confident.)

Maybe it's uncharitable for an adult to judge or condemn teenagers. But it takes superhuman effort to be charitable as one's daughter lies dying in a hospital bed, surrounded by those who had done nothing as she suffered, or even made that suffering worse.

They were the choir, that cacophony of voices who shamed and shunned her. The elementary school friend who had written on her Facebook wall: "Sluts are not welcome here." Great sobs moved over her chest like the crests of waves; her entire Facebook page, I later saw, became a memorial to Rae.

I wanted to rise up and decry them all — hypocrites, murderers, what right did they have, I wondered, to be here with us. But I didn't. Like Rae, they were children too.

For a while, in my mid-twenties, I went to the Halifax Shambhala Centre to study Buddhism and to pray. To the Buddhists I met, time was a construct, existing only in the mind. To a physicist, Rae had told me, time is relative to space and the velocity and mass of objects — in a black hole, the force of gravity may slow time to infinity.

Either conception of time was preferable to the linear hell I was living in. If I could transport myself to some earlier moment, what would it be? The beach in Mexico? The museum, warmed by Rae's giggles and the wonder in her wide child's eyes?

Or back further still, watching Rae's tiny infant hand slip into mine? Watching her take her first few steps in my parents' home in Ottawa. My father was still alive, and Rae stood up on those wobbly, stubby, pre-toddler legs, gripping his pant leg. She swung her head around, smiling, and stepped, delicately, despite her awkwardness, away from him and into my arms.

For the first few months after Rae was born, I lived with her and Leah. At first, I took fatherhood as a duty, changing diapers, providing financially, cleaning, cooking, always nervous, always waiting for what I would be asked to do next. Until one day Leah said, "Go out. Rae is yours, too. Take her somewhere. Enjoy her. Don't make fatherhood an obligation."

I nervously packed up Rae's diaper bag, a change of clothes, and some digestive cookies, and had Leah make up some bottles. We went to the Halifax Public Gardens. It was a sunny midsummer day, the boughs of the tall maple trees swaying in a warm breeze off the Atlantic Ocean, the roses and daisies opened up to the sun, the air light and warm with a soft, milky haze. That was the day fatherhood ceased to be mechanical for me. Rae and I played with her wooden toys and I watched her try to pull her torso up, her hands wrapped hard around the tray of her stroller. Even before she could walk, she seemed driven to explore the world.

The media descended late on Saturday.

First, the calls came to Leah. Local media, wanting to know more about her Facebook post, which, unbeknownst to us, had been reposted far and wide. Leah told them the whole awful story, starting with November 2011. How wherever Rae turned, no matter which fork in the road she tried to take, she was knocked back. The disloyalty, not just of the boys, but of the peers who stalked her from school to school, never giving Rae a moment's peace. Leah told the media how the police, after so long, had eventually closed Rae's file, and how the schools were unable to control the circulation of the photograph and the bullying, denying her a safe haven even there. Rae fought so hard to come back to us and to herself, but she was not only left to her own devices — to drugs, cutting, depression, panic attacks — but was in many ways actively thwarted in her recovery by those who should have helped her.

Before I made the trip to the hospital that Sunday morning, I sat in Rae's room and stared at her artwork, framed on the walls, including a pencil sketch of a tiger that I knew she had done while at 4 South.

Beside her bed, on a small table, was a notebook. I picked it up, the pages crinkling as I opened it slowly. It was her diary, her life, her memories. Any other time, I would have felt like I was intruding and not looked. But not now. It was, for me, Rae. I stopped where she had inserted trinkets from our trip to Cozumel into the spine: her plane ticket, her electronic room pass, some pesos and some coins. She'd written the room number and the name of the resort at the top of the page and, underneath, "Best Time of My Life."

"When I am in a bad place, I think of the beach in Cozumel and I imagine I'm on it," she had told me just a few weeks earlier.

When I returned to the hospital, the doctor pulled Leah and me into a room near the ICU. He told us that the hospital had found five donors, but unless Rae died in a few hours, her organs wouldn't be healthy enough to transplant. Whatever was left inside me escaped then. My first thought was that this wasn't real. That Rae would wake up and say she was hungry.

And then panic moved through me. Those organs were all that was left of Rae. Those organs had to live on. I knew it was what Rae would want. This was it. It was time.

Leah left the room first to be with Rae.

Krista held my hand and we followed. "I hope where you are going next is just as wonderful as Cozumel," I whispered, leaning down close, my lips touching Rae's ear, her soft, milky skin, still warm. "I'm sorry," I said, "so, so sorry I couldn't have helped you." And that's when the machines beeped, erratically, a few times.

A nurse came into the room, checked Rae's pulse, and then pressed the intercom for a doctor. People came and went.

Leah on one side of the bed holding one of Rae's hands, me on the other doing the same.

Rae passed then.

The last part of her brain died.

Within seconds.

Gone.

Like she knew if she hung on any longer, she'd be taking more than just herself.

Chapter Fifteen
Sunday, April 7, 2013

A doctor told Leah and me that we had to leave Rae's room in the ICU. Something was said about the urgency of harvesting Rae's organs. I don't remember the exact words. My child was dead. That was all that I was hearing.

Leah and I didn't move at first. We touched Rae, felt her, trying to freeze the moment in time, hoping for something to show us that she wasn't really gone. The machines were just machines, after all. Maybe they were faulty. Or maybe Leah and I stayed there because we wanted to believe so desperately that, while she had left physically, there was an afterlife, and Rae was there, finally, unscarred and happy. We just needed to know.

But we couldn't remain. The nurses were ushering us out.

Leaving that room was pulling me away from everything that remained of Rae, and I knew nothing would be left of me to continue on when I left. Krista had to carry me, one of my arms around her shoulders, the other drooping, my two-hundred-pound frame pulling down hard on tiny Krista's 130 pounds. In the elevator, I felt my chest contract and I struggled to breathe. My eyes watered as Krista moved me out of the hospital and to the hotel where Casey was staying.

The day before, Casey had slipped away from the hospital for a few hours to attend an Alcoholics Anonymous meeting. He was sober now, clean, and had given me his thirty-day sobriety coin. He said to me, "I have no answers. There is nothing right about any of this. You just tell me what you need. I am here for you." I moved the coin between my fingers. And while he didn't say so, I felt in his strength that what was to come next wasn't about me overcoming the death of Rae. She would always be a part of me, as would everything we'd gone through together. That coin symbolized the strength to move forward in the face of the worst darkness any parent would ever have to face. In Casey's room, my entire family from Ottawa, including my mother, were present. Someone handed me a glass of water, someone else took off my glasses and cleaned the steam from them, and someone else patted my back.

No one told me everything would be all right. I was glad for that, because nothing ever would be all right again.

The next day, Leah, Jason, Krista, and I started to make arrangements with the Atlantic Funeral Home for the burial. I was included in everything, but Leah was really making the decisions. We had decided we wanted to cremate Rae. But we all knew that Rae needed a tombstone as well, a resting place. We all wanted somewhere physical to go to remember.

We discussed wanting a small service, to be held at St. Mark's Anglican Church, where Leah's mom had sung soprano in the choir and Reverend Ron had preached for a bit. We wanted to celebrate Rae's life, her wonderful, probing, curious life, with family and a few close friends. Leah, Jason, and Krista did most of the talking at the funeral home. I wasn't really there, but I still can't tell you where I was. I was floating in time.

For a while, in my early twenties, before I met Leah, I was married to a woman who was part of a fundamentalist, evangelical church. In her church, hell was on earth and our liberation came from surrender and trust in God. I firmly believed Rae was in a safe place now, but we, left on earth to mourn her, were in that hell. I could not sleep, waking instantly after dozing with vivid memories, so heartbreaking, for even in the midst of those memories I knew she was gone. Krista had to help me get dressed in the mornings. She had to remind me that she was there, that there were things to do, that I couldn't disappear.

After the funeral home, Jason, Leah, Krista, and I walked to Dartmouth Memorial Gardens cemetery, looking for the perfect burial spot for Rae's ashes. As the four of us walked, I felt the cool spring air on my face, the wind nipping at the back of my neck, the crunch of new grass under my feet. Momentarily, I felt something transcendent move through me, a peace that I couldn't explain. I felt Rae was everywhere and I could feel her.

The funeral home director led us to a vacant spot near a young maple tree. I could hear birds chirping and a crow squawk. It seemed peaceful. I let out a sigh. I knew this was where Rae would want to be, beside a tree that would grow for years to come, where deer would prance when no one was around. All of us left feeling some kind of strange peace.

Later that day, though, the manager of the funeral home called Leah to say that the hospital wasn't releasing Rae's body. An autopsy needed to be performed, with a police officer present, on all bodies resulting from death by suicide. The four of us were still all together, now in Leah's home to talk about the funeral arrangements, but we had found ourselves sitting in silence. The kitchen counters and dining room tables were crowded with open Tupperware containers and foil trays of lasagnas, casseroles, salads, and meat dishes. Bouquets of flowers, plants, and cards lined every square inch of shelving. The neighbours and Leah's friends and even complete strangers had come out to help in their own ways, showing they were there. I was grateful, at the same time asking, ever so quietly, where they were when Rae was in trouble and needed their support.

Leah let out a shrill laugh when she heard that the police were not releasing the body. She finished the call with the funeral home and pounded the numbers for Sergeant Ron Legere, the boss of the lead investigator in Rae's case. "Where were you when she was alive?" she screamed into the receiver, echoing my own thoughts. "And now that she's dead, you're telling me the police won't let Rae come home? You bring her back now. Take care of this. Bring our daughter back, now. We're done."

Eventually, Krista and I went back to Armdale, having made plans with Leah and Jason to meet up again early the next morning. I took some sleeping pills that kept me asleep until dawn. Knowing better than to ever put my phone on silent mode again, I still nearly missed the repeated calls from Leah because of the medication. When I eventually picked up, she was breathless and speaking fast. Leah, I managed to pick up, had received a series of Facebook messages from a boy named Brandon. She had screenshot the conversation and forwarded it to me and then the police. With Leah still on the phone, I looked at my inbox and read. Anger, devastating sadness, and fury flooded over me.

Brandon's message to Leah was long, and filled in for us much of what Rae could never remember:

> While me and (Zachery) were in his room with Rae, we started doing things with her and she was OK with it (I am not the type to force sex upon anyone. I have to older sisters and I respect girls the way I would want them to be respected)...me and (Zachery) were having sex with her for a little bit and she was still OK with it but about 15 mins after (Amanda) left Rae looked like she was going to get sick. I asked her and she said she was good but then she started to quince a bit so I ran to (Zachery)'s window and opened it. We both helped her over so she could get sick. She was out of the window for about 5 mins and we were asking if she was OK, she said, "I'm fine you guys can keep going if you want." I told (Zachery) to go ahead and he then told me to go ahead, so when I went again, I'm not sure if it was my phone or his,

but the picture was taken without her noticing and me being a
drunk idiot I posed for the picture.
The other 2 boys are (Austin) and (Dylan) (Zachery's little
brother). We asked them to help us bring her to the spare
room so she could sleep there and (Zachery) could sleep
in his own bed. We woke her up and she didn't want to go
downstairs so (Austin) tried to pick her up and she hit him in
the face. Then we kept bugging her to get up and she finally
did and walked downstairs to the spare room.
She laid in the bed and it was just me and (Austin) and her.
Then (Austin), I remember, (Austin) telling her to kiss him and
she did, then he asked me to leave the room. I then left the
room and sat on the couch in the living room. About 20 mins
later (Austin) came out with a smirk on his face....

But for us, the most important parts of the message were the
admission that all four of the boys may have had sexual intercourse
with Rae, and that Brandon had distributed the photo afterwards.

I woke up the next day and was talking to (Zachery) and he
told me that she had sex with (Austin) and (Dylan).... Yes I will
admit to bragging about the picture for a few weeks and Yes I
did send it to some people. But please believe me that
I did not hurt your daughter that night.

Chapter Sixteen

Starting the morning after Rae's death, television crews descended from the major networks in Canada, the US, and beyond, reporters reaching out to Leah and me for comments, some even camping out on our front lawns or sneaking up our back gardens to get a picture of the bereaved parents. My voicemail was full, and text messages, social-media messages, and emails poured in. It was like a dam had broken way, with journalists wanting to hear Rae's story. But not all the messages were for interviews. Some were from Cole Harbour and Eastern Passage parents, angry at the publicity hounding them as well as us. Some blamed us for what happened to Rae, sending messages like this:

> Recent photos of Rehtaeh show her right arm tattooed up and a tongue stud which is used for oral sex...sometimes girls with low self-respect will assume the role of a slut. Is this what happened?

One parent, who kept sending Leah and me messages, said he was close with the boys and we had got it all wrong. In one of his messages, he wrote:

> She didn't report anything the next day and there's one reason for that. She stayed all night, enjoyed herself, stayed well into the next day and played video games She lied. She cried. She died. It's time to end the lies. Glen, it's time to tell the truth. ... It's beyond time to put this to bed.

And in another message he added:

> ...yes she was bullied...yes she died...all horrible...it
> never should have gone that far...but there was no rape, she
> should have been honest and sucked up the embarrassment.

Nova Scotia Premier Darrell Dexter contacted Leah and me, expressing condolences. The member of Parliament for Dartmouth–Cole
Harbour, Robert Chisholm, called for a moment of silence during a
parliamentary session in Ottawa. Before doing so, he said, "Everyone
has a role to play in preventing such a tragic series of events...schools,
law enforcement agencies, justice officials and indeed politicians, at
all levels of government, must do better. In honour of Rehtaeh Parsons
and anyone who has succumbed to the burden of victimization."

Canadian Prime Minister Stephen Harper's office reached out
to Leah and scheduled a meeting for us in Ottawa following Rae's
funeral. An assistant said the government had been looking at legis-
lation involving the dissemination of child pornography, including
pictures of kids taken by their peers and posted online. The prime
minister wanted us to speak to him about Rae's cyberbullying.

People I didn't even know — teenagers and adults — were coordin-
ating candlelight vigils, including one at Victoria Park, across the
street from the Halifax Public Gardens where I first took Rae as a
baby. It seemed as if the justice Rae sought in life might finally be
done.

In the days after Rae's death, but before her funeral, I began research-
ing teen assault cases, thinking that with all this outcry of support
coming from all over the world, maybe Rae was right. She wasn't
alone. I should have let her go to the media. Maybe she was just
a part of a much larger culture that silences victims and supports
victimizers.

I learned for the first time what I should have known already. I found the famous incident at Ohio's Steubenville High School that had taken place not quite a year earlier. In August 2012, a sixteen-year-old girl, the same age as Rae, attended a post-practice party for the Big Red high school football team. Steubenville is a small, dying steel town, where lives revolve around football. The victim, who was never named publicly, became intoxicated. Shuffled from party to party, she was sexually assaulted by partygoers, including football players, with the attacks filmed and photographed and broadcast across social media. Kids at other parties knew what was happening to this girl, in real time, and did nothing. During the assaults, not a single person tried to stop them.

The police in Steubenville worked quickly, however. Phones were confiscated, hundreds of thousands of electronic messages and images were taken as evidence. Ten days after the incident, two of the boys were arrested for penetrating the girl with their fingers while she was impaired, which by Ohio law is rape. The boys were convicted in March 2013, three weeks before Rae hung herself.

Like Rae, the girl in the Steubenville ordeal had woken up the next morning in a strange room, half clothed, her flip-flops, phone, and earrings missing, remembering little of the events of the night before, except that she had vomited.

What also emerged during the Steubenville investigation was that higher-ups, including the football coach, families, and possibly lawmakers and politicians, had tried to cover for the accused. "Boys will be boys" was the mentality of those who had the power to stop the attacks and raise their sons differently.

The mother of Audrie Pott, a fifteen-year-old California student who killed herself after an assault in September 2012, reached out to me. She said there were stunning similarities between what happened to Rae and Audrie. Audrie had been partying at a friend's house with boys and girls with whom she'd grown up and believed herself safe. These boys took her upstairs, assaulted her, and drew images of penises and the word *whore* on her body, then took pictures and distributed them. A little over a week later, Audrie hung herself. Audrie, like Rae, had shown no prior evidence of depression or suicidal ideation before the attacks.

Leah told me that, following Rae's death, Tiffany tracked down Leah to say that she'd lied to Rae when they had met a year earlier. Tiffany told Leah that everything Rae had heard about Tiffany being assaulted was actually true. But Tiffany didn't want to go through with a police investigation having seen the abuse endured by Rae.

I came to learn about the term toxic masculinity — aggression and bullying that have become normalized — and about how a default misogyny was embedded in institutions and social structures, unquestioned by men and women, boys and girls, who condemned victims instead.

It was a crash course that I wished I'd taken sooner. I wished I had not focused only on wanting Rae to get better and happier, but that I had been able to look more frankly at the darkness she was standing against. That darkness is within me too, within all of us, stemming from our culture, our parentage, our world. I started to blame myself, my own fears and insecurities, for not reaching out to other survivors when Rae needed to know she was one girl of thousands, not one girl alone.

The morning after one of the Thursday night vigils, Krista and I went for a walk downtown. I couldn't attend the vigils. I didn't have the strength, physically or emotionally, to be there. But as Krista and I walked on that sunny and crisp near-spring day, consciously or unconsciously I was moving us toward Victoria Park. Meandering, I eventually spied the monument for Scottish poet Robert Burns, where one of the vigils for Rae had taken place. (Nova Scotia is Latin for New Scotland, and its Scottish heritage remains a source of pride, with many Nova Scotians able to trace their lineage back to the Scottish settlers who arrived centuries prior.)

On, beside, and all around the monument were flowers, cards, and candles. A few were still lit, weak and dimming. There were pamphlets for those who lost someone to suicide. There were teddy bears.

I walked around the monument and stood staring at the Burns quote on the back: "Wee, modest, crimson-tippèd flow'r / Thou's met me in an evil hour," taken from the poem "To a Mountain Daisy."

Evil hour. I thought of the words on social media written about the victim of the Steubenville rape case:

> Some people deserve to be peed on

> Whore status

And Audrie Pott:

> Honestly like really no joke everyone knows.... u were one horny mofo.

And Rae:

> Sluts are not welcome here

I'd been drinking since I was a teenager — wine at dinner, beer with my navy mates. But now I was craving more. I marched home, so fast that Krista had to struggle to keep up. I poured myself a Scotch, the first stiff drink I'd had in months, not knowing that this would be the beginning of a long, dark tunnel.

I then sat down at my computer and looked at the blog I had started in the '90s, about technology, gadgets, and photography for other tech nerds like me. In the entire history of the blog, I had had maybe a hundred views. I thought of the power of social media to destroy lives; of the hundreds of thousands of images in just the Steubenville case alone that became evidence of rape.

But social media was only a tool. I knew how to use it too.

I wrote an entry titled "Rehtaeh Parsons Was My Daughter." My rant was directed toward Nova Scotia Justice Minister Ross Landry.

Within a few hours, Anonymous, the Internet activist organization, contacted me, having read my post. Some of the local members of the group saw it as a cry for help — and they saw the case as akin to the Steubenville case, which the group had also become involved with. In fact, the Anonymous hacker involved in the Steubenville case, Deric Lostutter, ended up facing more time in prison than the two accused rapists.

On April 10, 2013, Anonymous uploaded a video to YouTube, demanding that the RCMP lay charges against the boys, based on evidence of criminal wrongdoing they claimed to have uncovered. Anonymous went on to launch a Justice for Rehtaeh campaign, organizing protests in front of the headquarters of the Halifax Regional Police, and began forwarding Leah and me messages about that night sent between Cole Harbour kids, going back all the way to November 12, 2011.

#ItsOkayNotToBeOkay
Rehtaeh Parsons Was My Daughter

The worst nightmare of my life has just begun. I loved my beautiful baby with all my heart. She meant everything to me. I felt her heart beating in my soul from the moment she was born until the moment she died. We were a team. We were best pals. We often sat on my couch and laughed until we could hardly speak. When we weren't together she would call me or text me every single day, just to say hi, to say she loved me. The life I had with my daughter was a rare thing. It was wonderful, it consumed me. I was defined by it. It made my life rich and beautiful.

How is it possible for someone to leave a digital trail like that yet the RCMP don't have evidence of a crime? What were they looking for if photos and bragging weren't enough?...

Isn't the production and distribution of child porn a crime in this country? Numerous people were emailed that photo. The police have that information (or at least they told us they did). When someone claims they were raped is it normal to wait months before talking to the accused?...

My daughter wasn't bullied to death, she was disappointed to death. Disappointed in people she thought she could trust, her school, and the police. She was my daughter, but she was your daughter too.

Chapter Seventeen

Our demands are simple. We want the ends, the RCMP
to take immediate legal action against the individuals
in question.... We do not approve of vigilante justice as
some in the media claim. That would mean we approve
of violent actions against these rapists at the hands of an
unruly mob. What we want is justice. We are Anonymous.
We are legion. We do not forgive. We do not forget. Expect
us.

— "#OpJustice4Rehtaeh Statement Anonymous,"
Anonymous Canada, posted on YouTube, April 10,
2013

In 2007, when I was still with the navy but working part-time as a
photographer, I was sent out on assignment to cover a funeral. Two
teens had died in Dartmouth in a head-on collision. The photo editor
instructed me to sit in the church parking lot, with my camera and
super-long zoom lens, to get pictures of the family crying. I felt so
greasy, so horrible, doing this that I nearly quit my job. I had my
resignation letter all penned and ready to hand in when I remembered why I wanted to be a photojournalist. Just a few weeks earlier,
I had photographed the last survivor of the Halifax Explosion. In
December 1917, two ships, one laden with ammunition, collided in
Halifax Harbour, generating what was at the time the largest human-
caused explosion in history. The blast flattened much of Halifax

and Dartmouth and killed nearly two thousand people. This man's brother, asleep in his bedroom at the time, had been thrown right out of his second-storey window, dying instantly.

Chronicling stories like these made me proud of my job. Photographing that funeral, I felt, was the basest, lowest thing I had ever been asked to do. I was an interloper at a family's darkest time. I had no right to be there.

Maybe life was playing a cruel joke, bringing me full circle — *karma,* as Rae would call it. When I arrived at St. Mark's Anglican Church for her funeral, media was lined up, crammed and tripping over each other, cables and wires crisscrossing the ground leading to satellite vans. There were cameras pointed at us, on-air talent with microphones in hand, readying themselves to send back reports, and photographers fitted out with long lenses. The intimate funeral Leah and I had wanted had turned into a circus. The funeral's time and location had not been kept private, but we hadn't anticipated such an enormous turnout, including Premier Darrell Dexter and Halifax Mayor Mike Savage. We hadn't intended Rae's funeral to become a magnet for public figures. And we were dismayed, most of all, to see that many of the same peers who had shamed and abused Rae were there as well. It was standing room only. At least the pews in the front reserved for family were still free for us.

A bagpiper started the service, followed by the choir singing "Amazing Grace." Marianne read Leah's eulogy, while my sister-in-law, Shari, read the one I wrote. In part, it went:

> *I spent my life believing that the single most important thing a father can give his children is his time. There is nothing as important as that. That belief has now turned into a blessing as I look back on the many fond memories I have with my daughter. I have a lifetime of them. Her lifetime.*

I listened as the words I had written reverberated through the church. As I looked around at the crowd, I thought of that last living survivor of the Halifax Explosion. The original St. Mark's had been destroyed in the blast; the present building had been rebuilt in 1921. I was coming to see that the mind plays tricks on a person experiencing extreme grief: my thoughts would wander to the most trivial things, sometimes, like I had stored these memories away to dig out when the reality of my loss was just too much to bear.

In between the singing, the eulogies, the minister's words and sermon, the sound of a pin dropped would have echoed through the alabaster arches. At one point in the service, I stared up at the Gothic stained-glass window — its blues, yellows, greens, and reds — and wished I could disappear into it. I imagined it as a portal to a parallel universe; if I stepped through it, I'd be reunited with Rae.

After the service, my brothers — Jim and Casey — as well as Leah's brother, Stephen, and Iggy, a family friend, carried the casket containing Rae's ashes from the church. We walked beneath a dark, overcast sky, under a soft drizzle that misted our faces.

We managed to ditch the crowd of spectators and media, and no one followed us to the burial site.

Only Rae's two families were present, forming a circle around the hole in the ground, all of us averting our eyes from Rae's final resting place. Leah, Krista, Jason, and I had designed the tombstone together. "Forever Loved," we had written underneath a photograph of Rae. Etched into the black marble were sketches of Rae's childhood pets and two crows — Rae always said that she thought crows were speaking to her.

None of us seemed to know what to do at first, shuffling from foot to foot, our arms burdened with the stones, stuffed animals, and red and pink bouquets of roses we planned to leave by her tombstone. Finally, the funeral director stepped forward and said we should all say the Lord's Prayer.

Afterwards, one by one, we walked up to the cherrywood box that now held Rae.

When it was my turn, I put a hand on it, *on Rae,* on the box that contained her ashes; in my other hand, I held a pink stuffed teddy bear that I wanted buried with her.

"I am sorry I couldn't save you. I will miss you," I whispered.

There was an ocean of things I wanted to share with her — and I would go on to share them — but this was the most I could get out at that time.

Afterwards, Leah pointed up at a crow, watching and listening in a nearby tree.

The day after the funeral, my blog post, "Rehtaeh Parsons Was My Daughter," crashed.

I checked my website statistics and discovered that at any given time, more than forty thousand people were vying to read it. I could see that the media were the source of about half of the views: *People* magazine, *International Business Times, Huffington Post,* the *New York Times,* the *Globe and Mail.* I could also see the search engine referrals that were being used by non-media, the voyeurs, as I came to call them: "Rehtaeh Parsons rape photo," "Rehtaeh Parson's nude photo," "Rehtaeh Parsons porn."

Anonymous released another online statement claiming they would release the names of all four boys if the RCMP didn't reopen the case and charge them. Leah reached out to Anonymous, pleading with them not to do so. That wouldn't, she told them, be how Rae would have wanted justice.

Krista came into my home office at one point and dragged me to the TV: protests demanding the RCMP lay charges had erupted in front of the Halifax Regional Police headquarters. The crowd eventually began snaking its way through Halifax's downtown streets toward

Province House, the provincial legislature building. "I've never seen anything like this before!" Krista exclaimed.

Then the news moved on to other groups of protesters. One was called the We Are for the Boys Campaign. The other was Speak the Truth. Both groups were a mix of teens and their parents, protesting in support of the boys, and they had become vocal, not only out on the streets but also through blog posts and Facebook pages. They claimed Rae went to that house willingly, had sex voluntarily, and later falsely accused the boys of rape.

One morning shortly after Rae's death, I heard on the radio that Nova Scotia Justice Minister Ross Landry was not going to reopen the case. There is nothing, he had told the press, to indicate that police did not follow proper procedures. I sighed. I never believed he would.

But that same evening, listening to the radio again, I heard his position had changed. According to media reports, the justice minister had asked senior government officials to present options to review the case. I stood there motionless, unsure what to believe.

The following day, to my surprise, Chief Superintendent Roland Wells of the Halifax District RCMP dropped by my house. As I opened the door, I could see that his teenaged son was sitting in his car, a boy about Rae's age, his head lowered, his eyes downcast.

My first question was "Is it true? Is there a possibility the case will be reopened?" The chief superintendent shrugged and said it was possible.

I showed Chief Superintendent Wells into the living room. He took a seat in the chair that, just a few months earlier, held Rae's Christmas stocking and presents. I took a seat facing him, nervously perched on the edge of the couch where Rae and I would cuddle up, eat popcorn, and watch movies.

Chief Superintendent Wells began by apologizing for what happened to Rae. He said that the police force sent its thoughts and prayers. As he spoke, I couldn't help but think he was only there because, somewhere in Rae's file, there was evidence of police negligence. I thought back to the summer of 2012, and that meeting with Detective Constable Snair and Sergeant Legere. It seemed to me that they were covering each other's backs. Why else would the head of the Halifax District RCMP come to my house now? I was so skeptical by this point of anyone's sincerity or authenticity. I just wanted him to leave. But not before he read the messages from Brandon that had been sent to Leah.

With a shaking hand — wobbling from lack of sleep — I held out the messages that I had printed.

"Read it," I demanded, thrusting the papers toward him, my voice quavering. "Read it," I repeated.

He nodded slowly, took the letter, glanced at it, and passed it back.

"There is nothing in there we didn't know already," I recall him saying.

I found myself speechless, repeating his words in my head.

There was nothing in that letter the police didn't know already?

Chapter Eighteen

About a week after the funeral, Leah, Krista, Jason, and I flew to Ottawa for a meeting with Prime Minister Stephen Harper. Politicians, I had learned, were already focused on creating tougher and broader laws to deal with cyberbullying and harassment. The online distribution of sexual images of minors, and the pervasiveness of sexual assault among teens, were big concerns of the prime minister and his advisors. And not just girls, but boys as well, especially gay youth. The Prime Minister's Office wanted me and Leah to be part of that conversation.

In Ottawa, government agents escorted us to Parliament Hill's Centre Block. As we walked toward the entrance to the building, we were flanked by media — just as many journalists, and many of the same ones who attended Rae's funeral. Cameras were pushed toward us, and reporters asked for comment. The security personnel didn't want us to stop to answer, instead whisking us into the building and then to a boardroom on the second floor.

I sat down at the long wooden table and, swivelling around in my chair, I scanned the walls of the room. There was a photograph of a young Queen Elizabeth II, bookshelves lined with leather-bound books, and, inside a glass case, a vintage red coat, the uniform of the colonial British military. An inscription on the top read, "Love justice, you that are the rulers of the earth. — Wisdom of Solomon."

I sighed and shook my head. Our national and world history has always been about the exploitation of one group by another, the more powerful taking advantage of the less powerful, whether that exploitation be based on ethnicity, wealth, or gender.

We met first with Premier Darrell Dexter. He walked into the room and sat down at the boardroom table. He began talking, unprompted, about health-care funding, how it worked, how it was broken down. He didn't ask us how we were doing, or express his condolences in any way, and the interaction felt strange. Leah, Jason, Krista, and I gave each other sidelong glances. An aide brought the premier what looked like a submarine sandwich, and then turned to Leah and asked if the premier could accompany us into our meeting with the prime minister.

Leah had told me prior to the trip that the premier's office had, in fact, contacted her a few days earlier with the same request, arguing that his presence was needed to ensure any promises made by the prime minister would be kept. Leah and I had decided then that we didn't want to make Rae's death a pawn in a larger political game of egos. We just wanted justice, and to protect other victims, so Leah declined the invitation a second time.

Leah and I were eventually taken to the prime minister's office, being told beforehand that we should go in first, our partners after us.

I walked behind Leah, balling my hands into fists, willing myself to keep my mouth shut, to not say anything angry or sarcastic, knowing well enough that in my current emotional state, I was a short fuse that could cause more damage than hope. "Let Leah do the talking," I told myself over and over.

Prime Minister Stephen Harper stood up from behind his desk, which was flanked by two Canadian flags and pictures of his own children. He shook our hands and introduced us to the minister of national defence, Nova Scotia MP Peter MacKay, and the minister of justice, Rob Nicholson.

Harper discussed Canadian law around bullying and online harassment — how it could be changed and strengthened, and how Rae's story could help ensure no other child had to live through what she did. Leah and I sat beside each other on a leather couch.

The prime minister reiterated at one point what he had told the newspapers: "I think we've got to stop using the term *bullying* to describe some of these things. Bullying to me has a kind of connotation of kids misbehaving. What we are dealing with in some of these circumstances is simply criminal activity."

Leah talked about how frustrating it was that there were no laws in Canada that police could use to stop cyberbullying — what we didn't know then was that there were laws that could have been applied in Rae's case, but weren't.

I listened, I tried to pay attention, as Leah, the justice minister, and the prime minister talked, but all I could think was *let's stop the nice talk and get down to business. If we are here, let's make her death mean something. Let's do something, finally.*

Startled, I realized the prime minister was speaking to me. He told me that he and his wife, Laureen, had read my blog post. I nodded and focused on what he was saying: "I am a father. I can't imagine what it would be like for you. My kids are near the same age as Rehtaeh. If it could happen to Rehtaeh, it can happen to anyone."

I managed to croak out a thank you, for his understanding. But I really wanted to ask him if this was all just lip service.

Forty-five minutes later, Leah, Krista, Jason, and I left the prime minister's office. Back out in the courtyard, Leah, for the first time since Rae's death, looked to me to make a comment to the media instead of her. I stepped forward, as microphones were held up toward me and cameras turned on.

"It's frustrating for us to go through something like this and feel so defenceless to do anything at all to help our daughter," I said. "So we conveyed that message. We conveyed it very clearly."

A day later, back in Nova Scotia, I wanted to withdraw again from the world. I closed every blind and curtain in the house. I wanted to cocoon. At one point, I moved into Rae's bedroom.

Krista and I had left the room the way it had been. I was convinced we'd never move from the house, and I'd keep the room as a shrine of some kind. A part of me wanted to imagine that one day Rae would just come home. She'd walk into the house like she'd never left. Her hoodies and jackets still hung in the closet, the door slightly ajar. Her purses hung from pegs on the back of the door, like she would be back any moment.

I picked up a pillow, held it to my nose, and breathed in deeply, feeling the pain and panic move across my tightening chest as I realized Rae's smell was slowly leaving it. With that pillow and one of Rae's stuffed animals in my lap, I flipped through her *Wreck This Journal*, a book of guided journaling and art prompts, and then her Bible, having already scoured every page of her diary, looking for a note, a clue, a message, something to make sense of all of this, some last words to us.

There was nothing. It was like her life had just been cut off.

Leah was seeing crows. Like a whisper, soft feathers tickled her cheek. She could hear something I couldn't. She said she felt Rae with her when she walked.

Krista had given me Elisabeth Kübler-Ross's *On Death and Dying*, on the stages of grief: denial, anger, bargaining, depression, and acceptance. She was encouraging me to go to a grief counselling group session and meet other parents who had lost children, some to suicide. Because of the publicity surrounding Rae's death, I was getting emails from survivors' groups and counselling centres asking if I wanted to come to one of their sessions. Psychics were reaching out to me, too, finding me through the blog, saying they were talking to Rae:

She's in a peaceful place.
She's better off where she is.
She has a message for you: she is happy you are okay.

I laughed at that one. I was far from okay.

I kept seeing, in some blind fog, my father's turned back on those stairs, that image from so long ago, and berated myself, believing I had done the same to Rae. I turned my back on her. I should have done more, fought harder with the police, allowed Rae to go to the media. I felt I had broken the vow I had made to never be like my father.

I had more than one hundred thousand readers on my blog every day, but what was that when Rae wasn't here? What did it mean that the prime minister wanted to toughen laws to protect the Raes of the future? I was her father and I hadn't done enough when she was alive.

I grabbed a bottle of Scotch. Downed it. Then a bottle of red wine.

Then I went back to a message I had received from Anonymous, with the full names of the boys and the address of the house — that house. I had their identities, their location.

I drummed my fingers on my desk. I knew what I had to do. I hadn't wanted to know the boys' names. I was afraid of who I would become if I did know. But, like Rae, I had put my faith in systems that let her down.

Chapter Nineteen

My few days off at the Apple Store had turned into a short-term disability leave. On paper, for the insurance company, I was being given a few months to grieve. But I knew I wasn't going back to work. I had my navy pension. I would survive on that. I was unwinding, much like Rae had done. Now I understood her. Now I knew how easy it was to just lose yourself in your own spiralling thoughts. Like a loop, I was replaying everything that I could remember about my life with Rae.

Krista worked for one of Canada's large banks, which was head-quartered in Toronto, and she spent a few days there every month. In mid-May, she left me for a few days for a work trip, and in her absence I felt the void more than ever. To dull it, I drank. Hours, a night, days. I lost track of time, possessed, obsessed, hunched over the computer, screencapping everything I saw about Rae. It was like something had taken hold of me, something neurotic and self-sabotaging, but also a part of me.

I hope no other parent ever has to see, to live through, the kind of things I found online.

There were Facebook sites dedicated to shaming Rae in her death, like Rehtaehdedparsons, the profile picture being a photo of her face with a computer-generated image of a noose around her neck. People were writing on this site things like:

> We hung out and tipped a bottle because nothing of value
> was lost.

They were cheering for her death. Some of these were adults.

> I just wanna say that I am laughing at her death . . . fuck the
> Parsons.

> Lol she died.

> She died like a bitch.

> . . . lame ppl like her need to die.

There were memes, too, of Rae's face and the caption "hanging out at Rehtaeh's place" with pictures of nooses.

This post-death shaming wasn't just something that happened to Rae, either. There were websites set up dedicated to further humiliating Amanda Todd and Audrie Pott too, social-media accounts and memes celebrating their deaths.

On the Speak the Truth Facebook page there was comment after comment slamming Anonymous, calling the group Mouse for its sneaky, stealthy hacking of emails and social-media accounts. Speak the Truth argued that the public was only hearing Rae's side of the story. And the truth, in their eyes, was that Rae was a liar, an attention seeker, a child with mental-health issues who made everything up.

At one point, I know, I went downstairs and made half a pot of coffee, filling the other half with Scotch. I had forgotten all about Ozzie, who had peed in the house. I could smell the urine and I could hear him whimpering at the door, but I ignored him.

Back in the office, I recalled that Leah had confided what had happened to Rae to a friend of hers — a lifelong friend, like those girls Rae had met in kindergarten, with whom she'd made BFF necklaces on weekend sleepovers and sworn allegiance for the rest of their lives. Leah's friend, like so many, said she didn't want to get involved. She didn't want to express an opinion.

Online, though, many *were* taking sides, defending the boys. Protected from repercussions, sometimes by fake identities, they said what they dared not say in public.

> Keep ya head up guys@ This is outta control. The truth will
> come out!

> ...I think this "Rape" was actually a drunken sloppy night that
> she was embarrassed...

> ...maybe she could have not put several penises in her
> mouth that night...

By late afternoon, rain was falling hard, pattering on the windows and skylights. I ignored my phone and the messages from Krista and Leah: Krista checking in, worried, because I wasn't texting her like I usually did; Leah saying another anti-bullying organization, another media outlet, another politician wanted to speak to us. One of Leah's text messages said that the Prime Minister's Office had contacted her again. Stephen Harper was going to seek amendments to the Criminal Code to include cyberharassment, to give more and better tools for police to investigate and lay charges.

Blinded by fury and rage and alcohol, I screamed out, "But nothing will bring Rae back. Why does she have to be the martyr?"

I was so full of recrimination, toward myself, my own parents — my father — searching for someone to blame, someone *back, back, back* and buried deep down.

At one point, I lay down on the floor and stared up at the dome lamp on the ceiling. I closed my eyes and drifted. In between passing out and waking, I saw an image that seemed so familiar, but unplaceable. I was seven years old, lying in tall, swaying grass on the prairies, looking up at clouds sailing by, silhouetted by a hard blue sky. In one hand my camera, the other hand balling earth. I could feel myself breathing hard. I was hiding, escaping something.

When I woke up it was dark outside and dark in the house, Ozzie yelping at the door downstairs to be let out. I hadn't fed him since the day before.

Stumbling down the stairs, I opened the door and watched him do his business. I never let him out without his leash and a walk. But this time, I whistled for him to come back. Then I fumbled with a can of dog food. Unable to open the lid, I settled on giving Ozzie some leftover lasagna.

Later, out of Scotch, I grabbed a bottle of red wine and drank it quickly.

Knowing enough not to drive, I grabbed all the change I could for the bus.

On the bus, I remembered Rae telling me that the morning she woke up beside those boys, her clothes disheveled, her body sore, she had taken the bus home, all alone, abused, frightened, and not really knowing where she was or where she was going. My Peanut, my sweetheart, discarded and used, a solitary figure trying to find her way back. That's all she ever wanted: someone to show her how to come home.

I took the same bus routes Rae had taken, but in the opposite direction.

I was going to do what I should have from day one: I would handle the boys myself.

It was still pouring when I arrived in front of that house.

It was one of those spring downpours that floods sewers, basements, and river basins, the rain so heavy it's almost blinding. When Rae was little she would say of such rains, "the sky is giving earth a good long bath to clean away all the dirt from winter."

I stood behind an old, creaking maple tree, its leaves weighed down by the rain. I was wearing running shoes, the pair of jeans I had worn the day before and the day before that, a thin shirt, a wool sweater, and a baseball cap pulled down low. The hat was navy blue, dark, hiding my eyes. I had no raincoat. No umbrella. I should have been freezing, drenched the way I was, but I wasn't. My body didn't feel anything.

I saw shadows cross behind a shuttered window on the second floor. Dread moved through me: *Was that the window? The window where Rae leaned out and threw up?*

I realized with a jolt that I had been here before, with Rae, in the fall of 2012, just after the police informed us they were not pursuing sexual-assault or child-pornography charges. I berated myself for not picking up on the significance of this house then.

On that night, Rae and I had been out having french fries on the Eastern Passage boardwalk. In the summers, we would walk the boardwalk with ice-cream cones — her favourite flavour was pineapple crunch — and often we would talk about the time when I lived just up the road, in Cow Bay. I was still in the navy then, living in a flat, and she and I would walk down to the beach and collect stones and shells and look for hermit crabs and washed-up jellyfish and starfish. Once we found a dead lynx, and Rae was upset for the rest of the day.

Rae was in a good place — she was letting Leah and me in. She hid little from us, or so I thought.

Rae had asked me, on our drive home from the boardwalk, if we could take a detour. I had followed her instructions — turn right, then another left, right again — until she told me to stop. I pulled over. She got out, shut her door, and moved over to my side. She leaned back against the car. I thought she was looking at the sky, which on that night was clear and speckled with stars. I heard her sigh, and I moved my body so I could get a look at the side of her face. I thought I saw her skin twitch, a shiver run through her, and a shadow move over her. Then she shut her eyes and a peace fell on top of her like a blanket; a gentleness and serenity I had not seen since before that night.

When Rae got back into the car, I didn't ask why we were there. I merely said, "Where to next?": not putting anything together, nor wanting to. I was dictated by Rae's moods, and to have a contented Rae was to have an angel back among us.

Rae had returned to the scene of the crime. Her way of closure? I will never know because I never asked her. So many questions I never asked and should have.

I clenched my fists tight and took a step forward, kicking the now-empty whisky bottle that I had purchased en route.

I could hear my breathing, deep, filling up my chest cavity, my attention becoming focused and alert.

I began walking.

A car moved up the street.

I stopped in my tracks.

My legs wouldn't move. I told myself I didn't care if anyone saw me. This was my night. I would suffer the consequences and accept my fate, but I was going to confront these boys and their parents. I was going to serve justice the way I had seen it served growing up: with brawn and might. "Weaker people are weak because they don't fight back," a friend of my older brother, Steve, said to me when I was ten. "My dad says you've got to take what you want in this world. There's no such thing as handouts." He was picking on me, behind Steve's back, punching my stomach and pulling my hair. I had started to cry, and he called me a wimp because I wouldn't retaliate. He whispered: "You'll never be a real man."

My legs, standing there in front of the house, still would not move.

It was like I had locked-in syndrome. I could see and hear, but I had no control over any other part of my body. I watched the car splash a mist of water onto the grass beside the road, its headlights snaking their way through the rain toward me, silhouetting the trees.

I heard that hum, that bloody hum, which when I was diving deep down in the oceans filled me with so much awe. Now, it made me feel empty.

Then, as the lights moved on me, it was like, for a moment, the illumination was coming from above, not from the vehicle. While the light shrouded me, it carried a voice. Rae's voice.

Dad, I don't want this for you. I need my dad to be well. Go home.

Back in Armdale, dripping wet, I started to make dinner for Krista, who would be arriving home within the hour. Pools of water collected around my feet. My socks sloshed and made footprints on the hard-wood floor.

I swayed. I moaned. I couldn't get Rae's voice out of my head. I needed her. I wanted her. I started to talk to Ozzie about the meal I was preparing — chicken-vegetable kabobs — and turned to ask Rae what she wanted. It was as if she was right there.

"Did you want peppers on yours?"

I curled up in a fetal position on the couch and cried for the first time since the funeral, clutching a pillow to my chest. Ozzie came up beside me, stretched his body up from his hind legs to lick my hand. I pushed him away.

I only wanted Rae.

I ached.

Every part of me was in pain. I passed out then, cold, unaware when the fire and smoke detectors started blaring. I had left the kabobs on to burn.

Chapter Twenty

Police in Halifax say they have reopened their investigation in the Rehtaeh Parsons case after someone stepped forward and gave "new and credible information" about the allegations that the Nova Scotia teenager was gang-raped....

"We have information from a verifiable person that we can substantiate with more questions," said RCMP Corporal Scott MacRae, a spokesman for the Halifax Integrated Sexual Assault Investigation Team. "And we're still appealing to others that may be out there."

—"Police reopen investigation of Rehtaeh Parsons case," Tu Thanh Ha and Jane Taber, *Globe and Mail*, April 12, 2013

I woke the next morning on the living room couch. I had a searing migraine headache. I was blinded as my eyes hit the light streaming in the windows.

For a moment, I didn't know where I was. I rolled over and groaned, staring out over the living room at the legs of the dining-room chairs.

I hurt all over, as if I had been kicked and punched, parts of my body beaten so badly they were now pulp. Inside, though, I was hard, like cement.

I couldn't remember how I ended up like this. The previous forty-eight hours were a blank.

I heard Krista grinding some coffee beans and grimaced, the noise piercing my head. Ozzie's chain clanked against his metal bowl.

Then I remembered fragments, like trying to open the dog food can. Krista, of course, would have given Ozzie proper dog food, not human leftovers. My leftovers, from the meals that Krista had prepared the day before she left for her business trip to Toronto.

My eyes moved to a clear, blue recycling bag on the floor, not far away from me. It held empty liquor and wine bottles. I shivered, realizing what I'd had to drink in the past few days: a lot.

Krista was playing music, either from a radio or her iPhone. She usually listened to the CBC morning news, but it couldn't be that — the light shone in from the windows, it was probably well after noon.

On shaking, weak legs, I got up and made my way to the kitchen. I stood at the door frame and stared at the stove, burnt, and the countertop, with a used fire extinguisher sitting on it.

Krista's back stiffened. She didn't look at me.

She stopped cleaning and stood still as a statue. Even Ozzie seemed to become a fixture in a wax museum.

And that's when it all came back to me. All of it, the past two days: staggering out and taking a bus to that house.

"I...I...I..." I spluttered. My mouth was pasty. Krista was breathing heavily now. "I'm in trouble," I pushed out, my voice barely a whisper.

"I know," she whispered back. "I know."

Krista and I sat side by side, our knees touching, at Point Pleasant Park, a forested city park full of meandering trails just south of downtown Halifax, at the edge of the Atlantic Ocean. I was looking out over the grass as Ozzie ran back and forth, catching a tattered tennis ball that Krista and I took turns throwing. The day had turned overcast; black clouds coming off the Atlantic foretold another rainstorm was on its way. Around us were the reminders of 2003's Hurricane Juan: the dead trunks of massive trees felled in its winds. I took a breath, inhaling the sea and the scent of fresh earth.

Krista worked in talent development at the bank, and when the bank was about to release a new product, they would have Krista and her team design a training program for managers and frontline workers. Most of her team was based in the bank's downtown Toronto office, and rather than continue commuting between provinces, she brought up the idea of permanently moving to Toronto. There was no way I was leaving Nova Scotia, I snapped at her.

I listened to some preschool children cooing and laughing as they plucked dandelions and blew the fluff into the air. Some cyclists on the path not far from Krista and I called out to each other.

After a long sigh, her voice wavering, Krista continued, saying she had met with someone in Toronto, a psychologist. "He specializes in trauma, Glen," she said. "You need help. We're dying here." I could sense she was afraid that she was losing me, and the truth was: she was. I was losing myself.

"Jesse [Hanson] said he would see you," Krista continued. "He does the trauma work Rae had wanted..." Krista's voice trailed off.

I shook my head. "I don't want to see anybody."

"But you need to see someone," Krista said, pinching her eyes shut and balling her fists. She was angry too, angry with what I had become. "What about one of those group counselling sessions with other parents who have lost children?" she suggested after a short pause. I didn't look but I knew tears were streaming down Krista's face. "Can you try?" she asked, her voice shaking and desperate.

I thought back to one of the meetings Leah and I had attended with other parents whose children had been bullied and died by suicide. It wasn't a counselling session, but some event to raise awareness. A father had pulled me aside during a break and almost berated me, saying, "No one ever met with me when my daughter died. No one ever wanted to talk about my daughter's case. The media didn't contact me." I could understand his pain. I could feel his agony. No child should be forgotten. But what could I say to him? "Reaching out to other people for emotional help is hard for me," I told Krista.

And it was true. This was never more apparent than during the summer when I was twelve. I had joined the Air Cadets and was set to go on a two-week sleepover camp. When I arrived, I was told I couldn't take part after all because my thirteenth birthday was after the cut-off date. I had to be thirteen or older. It was an oversight on some administrator's part. I had to go home.

My mother and other siblings were in Toronto for the summer. My father was working long hours on the base. I had to entertain myself alone, making model airplanes and reading science-fiction novels: *I, Robot*; *Nineteen Eighty-Four*; *Alien*. One morning, after eating a bowl of cereal with spoiled milk, my head started to swoon. I raced to the sink to vomit, missing it by inches and spewing my insides all over the kitchen floor. My knees buckled. I slid to the ground. I tried to roll over to reach the phone on the wall but couldn't. I wanted my dad. I needed someone to help me. I thought I was dying.

That day, I lay on the floor. By evening, the nausea had passed. I stood up on weak legs and cleaned up the mess. When Dad came home with some fried chicken and french fries for us, he didn't know I'd been sick all day. I didn't tell him. It was an unspoken code between my father and his sons: don't complain. Suffer in silence.

Krista was finally touching me, stroking my hand and then looping her fingers through mine and squeezing tight. As she did, I felt the crushing weight of sadness inside me — I wanted her to hold me, but at the same time I felt so undeserving of her love. I wanted to be deserving. I tried to be. But no matter how fast I ran, there was something deep inside me that was ugly and hateful. Rae's death just unleashed that monster. Tears formed and I started to cry too.

"Look at what counselling did for Rae," I stammered.

We sat silently for what felt like hours but was probably only minutes.

"I'll see someone here," I finally acquiesced. "But not in Toronto." The thought of leaving even for a weekend, let alone moving, selling the house, packing up Rae's bedroom, being at a distance from the places Rae and I went to together — these things were all I had left of her, I told Krista. I couldn't say goodbye to that.

"Jesse deals with trauma. It's his specialty," Krista pressed. "And while my health plan from work wouldn't cover Rae, it does cover you as my husband. Jesse takes you back to where all the wounds were formed. You are not to blame, but you're carrying a lot of guilt. Maybe listen to Casey, talk to him about your alcohol use, about...about what he feels is your family's secret. Maybe that is what is tearing you up. He's clean now, you know."

I was set to snap again at Krista, reminding her that Rae's death was what was tearing me apart. But I stopped. "I won't call Casey," I said with a sigh. Casey was finally nearing a good place, a healthy place, and I wasn't going to be the one to drag him down again. In hindsight, though, I realized I hadn't wanted to speak to Casey. I wasn't ready to face the truth of what he would say.

When I was stationed in Fort Walton Beach, Florida, in 2003, our area was hit with the tail end of a hurricane two days after I arrived. Sirens blared, warning everyone to stay inside and close the metal hurricane shutters on the windows and doors. Before I did, I peered out the window and saw the street flooded with a fast-moving river. I have always been fascinated by the weather, by the power of storms and our frailty before them, the reminder that we are merely guests on this planet. No matter how hard we try to control anything, something more powerful can always sweep it away.

I was thinking about that trip — about Rae's visit, and her swim with the dolphin — on the same day I got the call from Sergeant Andrew Matthews of the Halifax Regional Police. He told me he was now in charge of Rae's case. He was calling Leah and me to introduce himself.

He began by telling me he knew I probably didn't have a lot of faith in the police at the moment — which was absolutely true — but he asked me to have some faith in him.

"He's got a fresh set of eyes," Leah texted me as Sergeant Matthews and I spoke.

He told me there was new evidence, and a statement was soon to be released to the press. He couldn't tell me more since it was an active investigation. But, he added suggestively, "you know."

I hung up and went to the nearby parkette with Ozzie, chain-smoking along the way, and when I got back, the reopening of Rae's case was on the news. "News sure gets around fast," I said out loud. I sank down on the couch with a bag of Doritos — I wasn't drinking during the day anymore, so I was gorging on junk food instead — and watched CBC's twenty-four-hour news channel. As I chewed, my mind stirred. The new evidence had to be that letter from Brandon, but then I remembered Chief Superintendent Wells's words: "There is nothing in there we didn't know already."

Then, Marilyn More, the lead minister on the Action Team on Sexual Violence and Bullying for the Nova Scotia government, ordered a different review of Rae's case to determine if school and mental health "policies and procedures related to bullying, cyber-bullying and sexual violence were followed." The review was also ordered to "identify issues in the school system and between schools and the health-care and justice systems" that might have a negative impact on a child's mental health.

Not long after that, Premier Darrell Dexter recommended an official judicial review of how Rae's case had been handled by the police. Former deputy attorney general of Ontario Murray Segal would later be contacted to conduct the review.

Rae's death *was* turning political, at home and internationally. I couldn't keep up with the text messages and phone calls. Leah was zinging me dates of conferences we were being asked to attend and speak at across North America, Europe, Australia, New Zealand.

People magazine did a big spread on Rae's story, and suddenly Leah and I had American anti-bullying, anti-sexual-violence, and anti-cyberbullying organizations begging us to speak. Leah was navigating this better than me. I was way out of my depth, hanging on like a sailor to a life ring I wasn't sure could hold my weight. For weeks, months, I languished, until I found my strength.

It was on a sleepy June afternoon. A local television station showed up for an interview I had forgotten I'd arranged. I led the broadcaster and the cameraman into the backyard to set up. The cameraman explained that it was a great place to film, the light perfect, a warm colour almost like custard. I wanted to tell him I knew that already. I used to do his job. I quickly changed into a laundered pinstripe shirt, combed my hair — greying a lot faster since Rae's death — and swirled Listerine in my mouth.

The broadcaster's questions started off pretty much like all the other questions that came hailing toward me:

"What are your thoughts on the judicial review?"

"What do you hope comes out of it?"

He didn't, thankfully, ask any of the foolish questions some others had, like, "How do you feel about your daughter's death?"

Instead, he asked a question no one else had. When I heard it, I shivered a bit. I realized this was the opening I was searching for: unconsciously, I had been prepared to answer this question for a while now and had been waiting for a journalist to go there.

"Was Rehtaeh ever in a mental health facility?" the broadcaster asked.

I nodded, slowly at first and then faster, before answering. "Yeah... yes. Putting Rae in there was the worst mistake of my life," I said, wiping a hand across my now perspiring face. As I spoke I remembered the pictures of goblins Rae had plastered on her room's wall, surrounded by those haunting words I'd heard her yell, written also in thick black marker: "Just Another Day in my Personal Hell."

"I believed I was taking my suicidal child to see professionals, people who help kids for a living," I said. "But in the weeks she was in there, I couldn't understand how Rae was getting worse."

I saw the dragons that had made Rae laugh at first, and then made her squeamish, on the wall leading to the elevators to 4 South. Dragons with horse heads, frog bodies, giraffe legs...distorted images. Not real, Rae had told me, covering her eyes. An illusion. "In China, the dragon symbolizes superpowers, wisdom, strength, and luck. But here they're all disfigured," Rae had told me. "Like this hospital is a cruel trick."

And it was, I told the broadcaster. I then moved on to tell him from start to finish what had happened to Rae at the facility.

When that television interview aired, the IWK Health Centre issued a statement denying that they strip-searched patients. That prompted a torrent of letters to the station, and then the newspapers, from patients and their families, including girls who had been on 4 South when Rae was there. They talked about how they were strip-searched too, or knew someone who was. Some were there that night and heard Rae's desperate cries for help. A CBC News article published on June 11, 2013 added further weight to these claims. It quoted a patient who had stayed on 4 South four years previously, saying that returning patients were routinely subject to strip searches.

Chapter Twenty-One

*People who don't expect justice don't have to suffer
disappointment.*
— Isaac Asimov, *The Robots of Dawn*

Krista and I stared at the middle-aged man in the brown tweed suit,
beard fuzz on his chin, sitting cross-legged across from us.

The psychiatrist I agreed to see met with both of us for my first
session. He was, for the first part of the hour with him, interested
in my history of medications. Not many, but they included some
antidepressants that my family doctor had put me on after Rae died.
The psychiatrist talked about medications that, after he got to know
me better, he might want to try instead. "I'll try," I replied. At that
point, I was ready to try just about anything.

The weather outside was balmy, the light lingering until well into
the evening, casting soft, melancholic gold-and-blue hues across
the city. It used to be my favourite time of day. Now I was finding
that beauty or light of any kind made me feel dark and distant, like
I was an interloper in a world I no longer was a part of. A week
earlier, Krista had taken a short business trip to San Diego. She had
sent me pictures of the Martin Luther King Jr. Promenade, a park
in the city dedicated to the American civil rights leader. I deleted
the pictures when I remembered how Rae found solace and peace
reading Dr. King's sayings. I knew Krista was trying to help, but I

didn't want it. "Don't send me anything anymore," I wrote Krista when she messaged me pictures of the West Coast sunset. "When I see something beautiful it reminds me that Rae can't share it."

I had been spending all of my days in my third-floor office — the windows closed, the drapes drawn, the overhead light either off or dimmed — creating a hermitage, a cave, closing myself off to anything except Rae and her life. Emerging to walk Ozzie, to eat a meal with Krista, or even to sleep an entire night, was like crossing some threshold that filled me with guilt.

At the computer, I would post on my blog.

In one post, I wrote about the hashtag #handsupforrehtaeh, which people young and old had attached to photo posts depicting themselves writing the hashtag on their arms in solidarity, seeking justice and raising awareness of rape culture. The campaign even attracted a few celebrities, including Jada Pinkett Smith.

Another blog post was titled "Thank you Anonymous." In it, I thanked the internet hacking group, since I believed they were the ones responsible for prompting the reopening of Rae's file.

I would also engage in lengthy online conversations with people like "Barry" from Edmonton. He had his own blog, a shrine to toxic masculinity, on which he wrote about high-profile cases of sexual assault, describing how the victims deserved to be raped. He wrote a lot about Rae and about me, accusing me of abusing her and turning her into "a slut." He wrote that she killed herself to get away from me and tagged me in all of his posts. "All those boys weren't nearly as good as your daddy," he wrote one time. He accused me of pimping Rae out. He claimed, among other things, to have a stack of naked photographs of Rae. I called the Edmonton police, who went to Barry's house. They contacted me the next day to say he had no photos; he was just looking for attention, and I was giving it to him. Barry told the police he just wanted to hurt me, but he wouldn't explain why. I later found out that he was trolling well-known feminist figures, too, threatening to track them down and rape them.

There could be a hundred, a thousand posts supporting Rae or expressing sympathy online, but I'd brood over the one by some sicko saying Rae had asked for it. I'd doze in my chair at all times of the day, woken intermittently by sharp daytime noises: a car backfiring, a siren, or the squeal of a child on the street. In that place between awake and asleep, I'd hear Rae's seven-year-old voice calling for her daddy. I'd jump out of the chair with a jolt, turn, and ask Rae what she wanted for lunch. "Do you want pizza, or to make some pasta?" I'd ask her. (Before her death, Rae had been experimenting with pasta sauces.) "Do you want to go for a walk downtown, or on the water-front?"

Then I'd look at my bookshelf, my sci-fi titles mixed in with the books I had bought online about troll culture, cybersecurity, and Anonymous. My desk was covered in newspaper and magazine clippings about Rae's story, and the walls of my office were flanked by Rae's school photos and pictures of our outings together.

Krista's voice brought my thoughts back to the present, and the psychiatric session. "I think you're obsessed with your blog," she was saying. I realized I had been daydreaming. I turned my head. Krista was looking at me, her eyes red and puffy.

"Um..." I started and stopped.

"Glen, I don't know if this is healthy." By which she meant: obsessively tracking the online chatter about Rae, including the most obscene and toxic commentary, personally engaging men who were declaring she had never been raped at all. "I think you're consumed. You're not..." She stopped suddenly, with a look like she was about to say something she'd regret.

"Not what?" I asked. I stared at Krista, her eyes narrowed. She shook her head slightly and pursed her lips, as if berating me. "Not what?" I asked more softly.

"You know you're not in a good place."

I tilted my head back, stared at the ceiling, and closed my eyes. I took a long breath. In front of my eyes flashed my tiny Rae, as a little

girl, when the tips of her hair were golden in summer, her eyes twink-
ling teal. In my mind I watched as she built sandcastles at Cozumel.
If only we had made it to summer, and that vacation I had wanted to
take her on. I had fantasies of alternate lives and futures — if we had
stayed on in the Caribbean. I could have opened a small computer
shop. The thought of what could have been crushed me.

"If I stop my blog, she dies. Rae dies," I murmured, lowering my
head and opening my eyes to see the psychiatrist jotting notes down
in a book.

I turned to Krista. Her body and face slackened. She knew. She
knew where I was going with this and, while she had her concerns, she
would support me. "I need to do this blog, for me," I said. I wanted to
cry, to break down. I had, no matter how much I cried, what felt like
a bottomless well of tears inside me. "I'm trying here," I pressed on. I
was spinning out of control, it's true, but I was afraid to stop. To stop
would be to look at the world and find Rae gone.

On August 8, 2013, Leah and I were called to a meeting at Halifax
Regional Police headquarters. Sergeant Matthews said he had news
and wanted to tell us first and in person.

I was sure I knew what was coming. I was certain that this was a
formality to tell us the charges were not going to be pursued. Leah
tried to convince me to have some faith.

Sergeant Matthews led Leah and me to a meeting room we'd never
been in before, on the second floor of the building, full of surveillance
and video equipment and cameras. As Sergeant Matthews conducted
the usual formalities, I sized up the equipment: this piece in good
shape, this one antiquated, and this one state of the art.

I had just given my notice at the Apple Store. I knew I couldn't
deal with customers anymore, people complaining about their broken
phones and computers. I knew I would be better off having left. I
would think about work and a job if I ever emerged from this tunnel.

"We'll be laying child pornography charges of production and distribution," Sergeant Matthews said. My eyes darted from the cameras to his face.

"What?" I exclaimed.

"We are laying charges against one of the boys for production of child pornography, and against another boy for distribution of that pornography," he said.

"The other boys? You couldn't find anything on them?" Leah asked. Matthews shook his head.

"What about sexual assault?" I cut in.

Matthews sighed and looked down at the file open in front of him.

"What about sexual assault?" I asked again. "Any charges going to be laid there?"

Matthews closed his eyes and let out another exhale. "Glen," he said, looking up, "that's just not going to happen."

Leah's shoulders shook and eventually her torso folded onto the table. I too felt that knot tightening in my chest. I wanted to crumble. My throat was dry. Around us was the hum of the station — electrical wires, feet rushing back and forth outside in the hallway, whispered conversations. Sergeant Matthews didn't say anything, but he also didn't look down. He was there. He was trying.

I reached over and rubbed Leah's back as she sobbed. One thing Rae had taught me is that crying was good. *Let it out*, Renee had told her. *Crying is healthy.*

"Why?" I finally asked.

"Because, Glen, Rae is dead," Leah exclaimed, her words garbled with mucus. She was absolutely broken. I envied her that. I still felt hard as cement. "Once Rae died her testimony was hearsay. She couldn't testify at her own trial. Her statements to the police would be inadmissible."

"Is that true?" I asked Sergeant Matthews. He didn't answer, but when Murray Segal released his report in 2015, he confirmed Leah was right.

"Glen," Sergeant Matthews finally spoke up, his voice calm but powerful as he touched the folders in front of him. "This may be no consolation, but I know that this file will change lives in Canada."

Following the 2013 charges against Zachery for creating child pornography, and Brandon for distribution, the case received yet another blizzard of press coverage. People seemed polarized, black and white: those who supported the boys, and those who supported Rae. The mainstream coverage was sympathetic to Rae. While the boys were minors, and their names couldn't be published by law, a judge further ordered a publication ban preventing the media from reporting Rae's name, as she was now considered a victim of child pornography. (The publication ban was later amended to allow for her name to be used, provided she was not disparaged.)

It upset Leah to learn that the boys were also being harassed, much as Rae had been. At first, I felt the boys deserved what they got, but eventually, I came over to Leah's perspective: a vigilante mob was not what Rae would have wanted. It was true. Rae had even said to me, "I just want an apology. I don't want their lives ruined, not like mine."

When I would become overheated, Krista and Leah tried to calm me down by telling me that the girls who shunned Rae, and the boys, were also victims. "The boys have been raised to objectify and demean girls and women," Leah would say. "They think a real man is all power, control, and being in charge, entitled to girls' bodies. And the girls are raised to accept it."

The boys were formally charged on August 8, 2013. Leah and I arrived at the courthouse early that day, to be there when the charges were read out.

Before we could reach the courtroom, Sergeant Matthews and the crown attorney whisked us into a side conference room. He told us that the evidence was overwhelming, and the boys had been advised to plead guilty.

I know I stared, for the longest time, in some trance between belief and disbelief.

Leah, in a shaky voice, managed to ask what I also wanted to know: What had changed? What new evidence had come to light?

"There is nothing in there we didn't know already," I said loudly, not sure where the words were coming from. "That's what I remember the RCMP chief superintendent told me when Rae died, when he came to my house."

I was directing my conversation now toward Sergeant Matthews. "He sat in my home and said there was nothing in that letter Brandon sent that they didn't know already. The only thing different," I lamented, my voice croaking, "is that it isn't just us that wants action. Now, the world wants answers and people taking responsibility."

Leah started to wail, but I pressed on.

"The police and your office had the same evidence when Rae was alive," I continued. "Why didn't you do anything then?"

The crown attorney said that the judicial review should give us the answers to our questions. All our questions.

As we walked into the courtroom, the father of one of the boys, a sister, and a posse of her friends wearing white T-shirts with Speak the Truth written on the front in pink, glared at us as Leah and I followed the crown attorney.

Leah, walking slowly — I worried her knees were going to fold at any moment — kept looking forward. I, however, kept glancing back, searching for some contrition in the faces of Rae's tormenters. Some vulnerability to show that they knew what they had done was wrong; that Leah was right, that they were victims too.

The boys sat in the box for the accused on the left side of the courtroom. They were dressed in suit pants and crisp button-down shirts. Zachery's eyes were looking down, his shoulders slumped.

His head, I thought, seemed to hang heavy. Maybe he was sorry, or embarrassed. Brandon, on the other hand, kept turning and winking, occasionally waving at his family, who were sitting behind us, and his other supporters.

When the judge read the charges out, Zachery's face flushed. Brandon's lips moved into a smirk. He caught me staring at him and quickly looked away, shaking his head slightly like this was my doing, my fault.

Leah got up first and read her victim-impact statement.

I followed Leah, addressing the boys directly, saying, "Rae told me one time that she would have forgiven you, if you only said you were sorry. It would have meant the world to her to have heard those words."

The judge wasn't easy on Zachery. "What would possess you to do something like that to someone?" he demanded. Zachery shook his bowed head and mumbled that he didn't know. The judge asked if Zachery had anything to say, anything to add. In a mousey, high-pitched voice, he whispered no.

Brandon, when it was his turn to address the judge, said in a loud voice that he would take responsibility for sending the picture around, but he didn't kill her. A hushed cheer erupted behind me from his fan club.

Outside the courthouse, the media scrum and members of Anonymous, wearing Guy Fawkes masks and beating drums, scurried up to me. I met them square on, taking one of the broadcasters' mics, and said:

> It took my daughter's death before the police would lay charges. That picture got my daughter beat to death, and now they're calling it child porn. If it's child porn now, it was then, too, when she was alive, when the police could have done something to save her. It's the same picture.

Chapter Twenty-Two

*There could be shadow galaxies, shadow stars, and even
shadow people.*
— *Brave New World with Stephen Hawking*

In the winter of 2017, Krista finally convinced me to sell the house
in Armdale and move to Toronto. She took her boss up on his offer
to relocate her to the bank's head office, and I was ready to do what
I once thought I would never be able to: clear out Rae's bedroom.
Halifax had turned dark for me. Just months before, I couldn't
imagine leaving the place where Rae and I had been together, but now
I found that everywhere I went carried too many painful memories.
It also had a fishbowl feel — I was too well-known; everywhere I
went people would point or stare at me or whisper as I walked past.
I wanted to fade into a crowd to mourn and grieve.

Before I packed up Rae's things, putting her books, clothes,
stuffed animals, diaries, paintings, and rock collections in cardboard
boxes and garment bags, I took photos so I could remember where
everything had been placed, where Rae had left it. Then Krista and
I took the boxes to Leah's for Rae's sisters to go through, to take
what mementos they wanted to hold on to. The rest would be stored
in the basement of the house that once belonged to Reverend Ron.
I gave Rae's bed to a charity shop because that is what she would have
wanted. But I told Krista I wanted to take her dresser with us. In

1997, when Rae was a toddler and I was in charge of the diving gear for my military unit, I had access to a truck. When I took my leave that year, I drove that truck to Ottawa to see my father. Together, we made Rae the dresser. It was thick pine, with a signature on the back: "To Rae, love Grandpa and Dad."

In the U-Haul that Krista and I would drive across Quebec, along the St. Lawrence River, and into Ontario, I put that dresser, as well as Rae's tall mirror. It still had the stickers on it that she'd begun collecting in elementary school: the names of her best friends, pictures of unicorns, that sort of thing.

I spent the days leading up to our move revisiting all the places Rae and I loved: the Eastern Passage boardwalk, Cow Bay, city beaches, the trails we used to hike, the pub Your Father's Moustache, where Rae would devour the fries, and the Halifax Public Gardens. After my first visit with Rae to the gardens, I began taking her there often. I would find a spot in the shade, spread out a blanket, and toss around her wooden toys. For hours, I would sit and play with her. Now I just stared out at the empty grass in front of me.

On the way out of the city, we visited Rae's grave, not knowing when we would return. The tombstone was flanked by bouquets of flowers, rocks with paintings and inscriptions like "I Miss You," and little stuffed animals and Kinder Eggs, which I knew her little sister Teaghan had placed there. There were also sealed envelopes, piles of them, that I suspected were apologies. I never opened them. It was not my place. But whomever left those, thank you.

At this point, I hadn't worked since Rae's death. It wasn't just the emotional toll. I honestly had little time between the speaking engagements, which I'd started not long after Rae's funeral, and which had grown in number over the years. Now pretty much every day I was fielding an inquiry, often from high schools or universities, to talk on gender violence. The travel and talks themselves took up a lot of time, as did the research I committed to — I felt a duty to the organizers to bring something more than my own sad story, and to try and express some insight, some wisdom.

I could get through the talks. But when audience members came to me afterwards, to express how brave they thought I was for speaking out — for trying to connect Rae's story to the pervasiveness and history of misogyny and rape culture, which created both the conditions for sexual violence and the culture of victim blaming and shaming, I felt like a fraud. I'd chew the inside of my mouth the way Rae used to, palms sweaty, just waiting to get outside and smoke.

After every talk, women and girls would approach me and say that they had experienced something like what Rae did. I was dumbfounded by the sheer number, and by the surprising number of boys as well, who said that they had been raped. Why didn't I know this? Why did so many suffer in silence?

And there were perpetrators too. Like the stocky, black-haired guy at one talk, who confided — in me, for some reason — that he had assaulted his girlfriend when they were both drunk. He was being honest, and he was ashamed. But I wanted to flatten him right then and there. I was squeezing my fists together, ready to deck him, as he told me his story. I looked at him and saw, in his dimples and dark brown eyes, a Brandon or an Austin, a Zachery or a Dylan. "You picked the wrong person to tell," I nearly told him, but I didn't. I waited until he finished and told him that he needed to own up and do something about it, and admit what he had done to others. I wasn't the man to give him absolution.

I was being touted as a changemaker and an activist but, to be honest, that wasn't what I wanted. I only wanted Rae back. Speaking about her, and about what happened to her, was a way of keeping her in the world, especially in the years before I moved to Toronto and found therapy.

When I agreed to go to therapy with Jesse Hanson, the trauma counsellor, I convinced myself that it was because I wanted to know what Rae might have experienced had she stayed with Renee at Avalon. It had become clearer to me that I was hiding; that the anger and hatred I harboured toward those boys, their supporters, the police, the world that failed Rae, had become a mirror in which I saw myself. It was me. I hated me.

After the charges were read in court, the fog lifted a little, I think. My obsession with Rae was replaced by something else, though equally haunting. I began to see flashes of some long-ago incident, something I knew was real but couldn't describe. I saw stairs, a familiar man's back, a feeling of someone's touch. In fact, the day after charges were laid against the boys, I told Krista that I thought something had happened to me too.

Jesse Hanson's midtown Toronto office was a far cry from the shrinks' offices I'd seen before. Jesse was known for alternative therapeutic styles and a focus on trauma. His office was sparse but comfortable. The lighting was soft, the background music leaned toward New Age, and the walls were adorned with Australian Aboriginal art.

He greeted me with a handshake and a smile. He looked like he'd just stepped off the beach after a day of surfing. A cynic might have looked at his office, his alternative therapies, his shoulder-length hair, and scoffed. But I felt relief. He was inviting and warm, an open book, and I felt I could be too. And after the endless and unproductive talk therapies I'd engaged in before that point, there was no reason not to try something different.

When he was in his early twenties, Jesse had been a holistic counsellor in Los Angeles, with a focus on yoga, diet, meditation, and exercise. He told me that in the course of his work he found clients connecting with parts of their psyche they didn't expect: the wounded children, angry teens, insecure adults. The technique he uses is known as somatic therapy, from the Greek *soma* — living body. The idea behind it is that our bodies retain past traumas, which manifest in years to come as pain, addiction, depression, and even physical illnesses and diseases.

"Trauma is not the thing that happened to us, it's the relationship we create to those events," Jesse explained. "Somatic therapies help patients connect to their bodies, see how they are carrying traumatic residue, and learn how to release it from the mind and body."

"What does this have to do with Rae?" I asked in our first session. "I'm here because of the stages of grief a parent goes through when a child dies. I'm stuck on anger."

"Glen," Jesse began, slipping forward in his chair. For a moment, I was taken aback, like suddenly I was naked in front of this man; that he knew more about me than I did myself. "I think you were angry a long time before all of this."

In my first sessions with Jesse, he took me through guided meditations to find a safe place — as Rae had done in her first sessions with Renee. This was where, he explained, I could return at any time if I felt afraid, overwhelmed, panicked.

My mind automatically went to the prairies, to the tall, parched grass swaying in the hot summer wind. I imagined birdsong, lying on my back and looking at the clear blue sky and a jet contrail. One hand clutched my first 35 mm camera to my chest, the other hand balling up the soil.

In another session, Jesse told me to imagine myself as a bird, flying high above — what did I see if I looked down at this scene? The answer surprised me: a child, seven or eight, wearing navy shorts and a grey T-shirt. But it wasn't me. The child was happy, I could feel, and I wondered if this was Steve, my brother. Jesse figured this was a problem. If I couldn't put my own face to my own memories, in what was supposed to be a safe place, a refuge, there was something in my childhood I didn't accept. Whatever it was, Jesse said, contained so much pain that I had to put it, and whatever part of myself it carried, somewhere I couldn't access. Such pain, he said, that I had to put it and therefore a part of me somewhere else, somewhere forgotten. But for my healing, I had to integrate that part of me that I'd disassociated from. I had to bring it back.

So this was where we had to start. Not with Rae, but in this field in the prairies. I knew where this would lead — a part of me had always known. But I was deathly afraid.

No matter how many times we went to that field in those first months, it was some other child there, never me. Jesse once asked me to see myself there as a man, an adult; I saw a grotesque figure, covered in welts and boils, skin scarlet red. I nearly vomited at the end of that session. It was how I saw myself: melted. So we changed tack and began in adulthood, moving backwards. It wasn't strictly as talk therapy, but involved meditation and a technique known as Eye Movement Desensitization Reprocessing (EMDR), developed in the '80s to treat those with PTSD and anxiety disorders. EMDR invites clients to focus on the cause of their anxiety, while moving their eyes back and forth, almost hypnotically. In my case, it felt as if my eyes reached a position where the memories and the pain in my body were the strongest. I would go deeply into those memories and feelings, as if reliving the experiences all over again.

I started in my twenties, during my first marriage. I believed my wife was unfaithful. I had joined her evangelical church, and when I confronted her about my suspicions she solicited the help of our spiritual leaders. They wanted me to endure — citing scriptures that implied marriage was for life and ordained by God — and I did just that. Years later, I reached the conclusion I had been "gaslighted" or subtly manipulated, a form of emotional abuse involving put-downs, passive-aggressive behaviour, and manipulation, to the point that the other person feels completely to blame for any breakdowns. When I finally left that relationship, I doubted my own self-worth. It was the first time I felt that way in my life, I told Jesse. But he doubted that.

Jesse had me go further back in time. Surprisingly, what I first recalled was when I was, maybe, in grade 6. Another boy and I chased a girl we knew around the schoolyard until she fell to the ground, giggling, and then let us grope her breasts. Afterwards, she stood up and smiled, and the other boy and I high-fived each other.

And then another incident, in grade 8, at a school dance. I learned that a girl got drunk and began throwing up in the parking lot while several boys watched. I was told that some people saw her having her clothes removed, and some boys pushing her to a darkened part of the parking lot. Several days later, I caught sight of her in the principal's office with her father. She was crying, and he was red-faced, seeming to shrink into himself from shame. The girl never returned to school. The boys weren't held accountable. Instead, she was sent away.

In both of these incidents, I saw boys — including myself — normalizing and excusing male aggression. And I saw how my self-esteem felt somehow bolstered in doing so. I already felt shame — from where I did not know. I hated who I was as early as elementary school. But somehow, in seeing someone made more vulnerable than me, my self-esteem increased. To be able to exert my power as a male, particularly a white male, felt invigorating.

Jesse was right when he said that I entered that marriage already damaged, or else I would not have been attracted to someone who would abuse me. But he reminded me not to cast judgment. Hurt people hurt people, he said. She, too, was unhealthy, to engage in such behaviour to control me. Something, somewhere in her life, felt out of control, and my first wife picked me to find that semblance of normalcy. Perhaps she too had been abused, and her way of coping was to control others.

Seeing this, putting it together in my mind, like pieces of a puzzle I'd been labouring over my entire life, brought up so much guilt. I lamented to Jesse that if I had understood, done this therapy, before

Rae even came into this world, I would have done so many things differently. Foremost, I would have spent hours talking with Rae, educating her, having her see how male dominance, male entitlement, had hurt and deformed all of us — males and females alike. Instead, I, as the masculine in her life, denied that there were problems. She went to that house trusting she would be safe, trusting that whatever happened between her and the boys would be some mild flirtation, at most, and trusting the friend who took her there. She was that girl in the playground. She was the girl in the parking lot.

It was December 2017, a few days after what would have been Rae's twenty-second birthday. If she'd been alive, would she just be finishing university? Would she be on her way to hold a PhD in some science, or a law degree? I would never know. Rae's birthdays, even over time, never get easier. I cry on that day. I meditate on what she might have been in this world and who she might have become.

I cancelled a few of my sessions with Jesse, unable to do much but walk Alice, another pug that Krista and I bought for a playmate for Ozzie.

Then the anguish passed, enough that I could get back to my therapy.

When we resumed our sessions, I knew we were going deep, to the source of all that pain. Maybe that's why I'd wanted to take a break — I needed to be ready.

Jesse had me leave the prairie field to see why a child would hide there.

So I started. I retraced my steps.

Slowly, along the twisting dirt path leading away from the field, the warm smell of wheat floating over me, my bare feet covered in dust, I found my way to the asphalt roads of the military subdivision of concrete two-storey houses.

I saw our door. I pushed it open.

Unlike outdoors, bright and sun-drenched, I entered a realm of greys and blacks. The kitchen table was covered in food, a cereal box opened, a milk carton overturned, spilling its contents to the linoleum floor. The room smelled of unwashed clothes.

Jesse asked me to walk further, toward the wooden stairs to the basement, the stairs creaking, the paint peeling. In Jesse's office, I curled my legs up on the chair, like a child would do, sitting on the floor. I found myself short of breath.

Step after step, Jesse assured me that whatever I would experience, he would be there. I visualized going down. Until I saw myself, a seven-year-old child, naked.

And a relative was there too — naked, making me do things to him. I heard him saying to me, "close your eyes."

I was terrified. I wanted my siblings to come. My heart raced. I didn't know what my relative was asking me to do. I didn't know what I was doing. I just knew, I just felt, like it was so wrong and dirty. I felt so dirty. So ashamed.

Then I heard a noise. Light streamed into the basement from up above.

I looked up and saw that the door was open, and a shadow was walking down toward me.

When his face came into focus, I could see it was my father.

But when his eyes caught mine, he turned, and walked back up the stairs, away. I reached for his broad, strong back to help me. Instead, he — my father — left me in the hands of a monster.

Casey had always said that a relative had molested him, *us, probably all of us*. He had turned to alcohol to numb the memories, he had said. I always knew Casey was right, but I had spent my entire life trying not to acknowledge it, not to look down those stairs. But once

I did it all came back. I even remembered how my relative was able to get away with what he did. My brother Steve was in the hospital for a leg infection. The relative had come to stay to look after the rest of us while my mother watched over Steve and my father worked. We were fodder for my relative's awful impulses.

After I came to terms with this memory, I looked back at Rae. When I saw her for the first time after that night, folded up on the couch in Marianne's house, all life inside her seeming to have been exhaled, I realized that I was also seeing me, that same wounded child. And instead of being her protector, of fighting back, I froze, like I did as a child.

We have several responses to trauma, Jesse explained: fight, flight, or freeze. I couldn't do what Rae needed me to do because I was still frozen myself. In a twisted way, I was blaming myself, even though I knew the relative betrayed me. It was like my abuser chose me because I was weak and ugly. If I had been better, he would not have hurt me.

And, just like Rae, the one person I wanted so desperately to stand up for me, to show me how to live in this world, was my father.

And there was my guilt, my rage, and my anger. Jesse was right. I had been angry my entire life, burdened with the shame that my relative did this to me, and that my own father had been culpable in that assault and humiliation. Part of me still lived in that basement. My entire life had been shaped by my father's betrayal.

For most of my childhood, I believed I would be like my father, Thornton Canning. I thought that my life would be an extension of who and what he was: respected among his peers, a masculine figure in his home and community. We were never close, though, and as I moved into my teenage years, I believed the emotional and physical distance between my father and I was my fault. I was never athletic, never popular with girls, never handsome like my brothers. So I had made it a childhood mission to be accepted by him. When we lived in Cold Lake, Alberta, he would spend many holidays and weekends alone, or with other military men, on hunting trips, stalking wildlife and drinking rye. When he was gone my brothers and I would play in the basement where dad stored his guns and ammunition. I'd load the guns and *bang*, pretend to shoot. I imagined my father looking over my shoulder, smiling, proud of my kill.

As a teenager, I subscribed to *Outdoor Life* magazine, and would lay under the covers at night, reading about hunters lost in the woods, attacked by bears, surviving against the elements. I'd look at pictures of fishing gear and guns. I would daydream of the day I could go hunting with Dad.

When we lived in St. Louis, I worked in a restaurant called The Loft. I was a busboy, but I got a share of the tips, and over time I saved a few hundred dollars — a good sum for a teenager in 1980. I was going to buy my own rifle, get a hunting license, and join my dad on his trips.

I was very proud on the evening when I finally told him this plan. It must have been late, around 11 p.m., because I heard the theme music for the NBC evening news in the background. Early spring, too, because I was thinking that we'd head out to hunt deer when the season opened.

After I spoke, he grew solemn and serious. He didn't say much and spent two days mostly ignoring me. Eventually, three days later, he slipped into my bedroom late in the evening and sat on the corner of my bed, his big frame bending the mattress so much that I slid toward him. He told me then that I was a quiet one, unlike my brothers, who were outgoing; more like the men with whom he worked, more like his own father. I preferred to be alone, and he worried that, because of that, I was emotionally unstable. He worried that if I had a rifle, I might flip out and start blowing people away.

He then got up and left the room.

Nothing in my life to that point shattered me more. I was the reason that my father and I couldn't go hunting together. I wasn't manly enough and, because of that, there was something broken in me. At least that was what I thought until Rae's death. Now I was starting to see something else.

Neither one of my parents were healthy role models. My father gave my mother little freedom and little to no voice or decision-making, just like his mother had had. Her only power seemed, to me, to come when she was with the other army wives, playing bridge or other card games in the afternoons when their husbands were at work. There, these women talked about other women they knew: single moms and secretaries at the base, referring to them as loose and threats to their marriages. It was only in their tight-knit wife groups where my mother and the other army wives could make decisions — including which girls were acceptable for their sons to date and which ones were not. From what I could see, it was then, and only then, that these women had any control over their lives and that control appeared to revolve around excluding other women. I'd even overhear some of the army wives talking about how they had to submit sexually to their husbands; they had no choice to say no.

In my sessions with Jesse, I came to recognize that my mother and father represented very distorted images of male and female figures in our society. The boys and girls who'd tormented Rae were merely a new iteration of those same figures, representing who was accepted and who was excluded.

It was Leah's dad, Rae's grandpappy, who provided me with the most direction — not just about the kind of father I wanted to be, but the kind of man I wanted to be. He had been a sniper during the Korean War. He told me that when he returned to his home in Corner Brook, Newfoundland, he was broken, consumed with the guilt of all he had done and seen. He showed his vulnerability. But he explained that most men were taught very early on to suppress their emotions. As he once told me, we as a society can't tolerate seeing weakness, especially in our soldiers. Reverend Ron said he faced a choice: become angry and stoic and hide away the hurt, or put his fury and tears into something worthwhile. He did so through spirituality, being of service to others, and became a minister in the Anglican Church of Canada.

By the 1950s, plenty of fishing-dependent communities on the East Coast were dying — stores and homes were boarded up and people were leaving, blown asunder by the prevailing wind of defeat that comes with massive unemployment. Huge trawlers, big ships with nets that could scrape the bottom of the seas, and freezer holds that could enable them to stay out for months at a time, threatened to both wipe out work for the fishermen and destroy entire ecosystems.

Working on Nova Scotia's hardscrabble eastern shore and up toward Cape Breton, Reverend Ron became close to fishermen in communities like these. They asked Reverend Ron to start preaching and told him that they needed faith and trust in something higher to get through. For me, Reverend Ron represented an intellectual, spiritual leader, a man who served others, a man unafraid to hold and express the myriad emotions inside and around him. Compared to my father, he was a far stronger man in my eyes, unafraid to embrace his own weaknesses and follow his own life path.

My sessions with Jesse unfolded over the next two and a half years, my life laid out in front of me like I was experiencing everything all over again. One day, I mustered the courage to start the story of Rae, beginning with that 2011 trip to Cozumel and our conversations about parallel universes.

After sharing Rae's story, I told Jesse I wanted to connect with the boys — not in life, of course, but emotionally and mentally. I wanted to believe they were victims too, and I wanted to understand them. I pictured them in front of me, or at least what I recalled them looking like after seeing them in court. I felt the anger inside me, the hate and hurt. I wanted to kill them. But Jesse had me stick to the image, and slowly the hatred turned to something else. I saw their broken selves — not necessarily unlike me, hurt, trying to find their way in a culture that fostered one narrow path for boys. I saw their wounded lives in front of me. Like my father, they knew nothing but what they had been shown. "I forgive you," I whispered out loud, my eyes closed. "Most of all I forgive myself for holding on so tight to my hatred of you."

Jesse asked me to connect with Rae next. I couldn't. Just thinking of her intensified a need to hold her, hear her, feel her physical presence. I couldn't let go and surrender to anything less. But Leah could. She saw her in dreams, in her garden, even believed she could feel her in animals.

"I can't let go," I told Jesse after several attempts to visualize Rae. Every part of my body hurt when I thought of her, but I wanted to feel that pain. "If I don't feel agony, I don't feel Rae anymore. I think," I spluttered, "I think my broken heart is all I have of her and I don't want to give that up." I continued, crying. "Rae once told me she was afraid she would disappear into a black hole and be nothing, that her life would be nothing, like she never existed. If I let go of the pain, I'm afraid she'll be right."

The call came in late, just as Krista and I were heading to bed. Just that day we had cancelled our summer vacation to Rome due to COVID-19. It was nearing the end of February 2020, Italy was in lockdown and we had no idea the pandemic would soon close off much of the world. So when I heard Jesse's voice on the other end of the line, asking if I was available for a very short-notice trip to Costa Rica to take part in a retreat — a therapeutic deep dive using psychedelic mushroom therapy — I jumped at the opportunity. It was Thursday; the plane was leaving Saturday.

Despite all of the trauma work and therapy I had done, I was stuck on saying goodbye to Rae. I didn't want to. Jesse said that was more than okay. I could take as long as I needed to accept that she was gone, and if I never did, that was okay too. Instead, he had given me enough tools to calm myself when I felt that anger rise, and to incorporate prayer back into my life — some form of trust in a higher power or a power beyond ourselves. Like in my earlier life, I returned to Buddhism.

Ten of us would be on the retreat, the patients all dealing with an immense burden of some sort or another, accompanied by a handful of counsellors, including Jesse.

Arriving at the hotel was like stepping back in time to Cozumel. The scents, the sounds. There were even puppies running around the lobby, dogs that reminded me of Rae's Jasper and Ozzie.

On the first morning, Jesse asked each of us to come up with a word to describe why we were there. One word. I thought of *surrender*. I wanted to be free from the pain of loss and grief. I wanted to just let go of the fear that if I did, Rae would be no more. I knew the holding on was killing me and I knew I wasn't really guiding the audiences who came to hear me speak when I was still drowning inside. Most of all, I knew I wasn't honouring Rae anymore by clinging to her so tightly. After all it wasn't Rae, really, that I was stuck on. It was her death. She would have wanted me to remember her life.

The schedule was a series of therapy sessions, group and one-on-one, leading up to the day we would use mushrooms under the supervision of doctors.

Even in the navy, there were always drugs around, but I never did much except smoke the occasional joint. I was apprehensive about mushrooms, but I had been reading up on how ayahuasca, a psychoactive plant mixture used historically by shamans in South America, was now being used in therapeutic settings to release trauma with great success. The altered states of consciousness, hallucinations, and out-of-body experiences induced by these kinds of drugs reminded me of something like the parallel universes Rae was so obsessed by — a different experience of reality, concurrent with our own.

The setting for our use of mushrooms was perfect: the outskirts of a small village called Hacienda Vieja. We sat in an unwalled hut, surrounded by mountains and the sounds of the jungle. We started the ceremony with breathing exercises, chanting, and then meditations.

It would be nice to write about how I saw Rae, smiling, in some serene setting with flowers, shrouded in a white haze — my image of heaven. I guess that's what I went to Costa Rica expecting. It would be nice to say she gave me a message. But nothing could have readied me for what was waiting.

After I was given the mushroom ball, I lay down on my back on a mat and looked up at the hut's grass thatched roof. Soon, the colours of the world faded. Everything turned grey and brown.

I looked out at the sky, and the clouds passing, when one of them suddenly turned into a crow. The crow turned toward me and stared, its two eyes cutting right into me like knives. Then it faded and returned as a human skull, empty holes for eyes. Below the skull, the spine was still attached, chunks of decomposing flesh still hanging from it. There was no turning this off so I just stared at it, whatever the hell it was.

I closed my eyes and felt myself fading right into a fire, a funeral fire…*the fire*, I realized, in which we had burned Rae. I was in the crematorium with Rae, holding her tight as she burned.

Then, as quick as this image came, another followed. I was standing in Leah's house. Rae had locked herself in the bathroom. I saw Jason pounding on the door, kicking it in. I was there, in my mind, seeing it all.

and then silence.

The house was now empty. Medical gloves were strewn on the floor and the furniture was pushed aside. Rae had been taken to the hospital.

The bathroom door was slightly ajar.

I walked toward it.

I saw her glasses sitting on the counter.

I pushed the door open and gasped.

She was there. Rae. Tall and beautiful, whole and as graceful as I ever remembered. I think I started to cry. In my head I was yelling at her to stay. *Please stay. Don't leave.*

But she walked past me, a ghostly presence. She didn't even seem to see me.

I followed her outside. There she turned into ash and was blown up into the wind. She became the sky, which was now blue again, the colours returned.

I felt a calm come over me like I don't think I have ever experienced in my life. A peace. I whispered goodbye into the wind.

The entire journey, I later learned, lasted four hours. After, I lay down on the mat and cried for several more. All of us did as all of us were lost in our own experiences.

We finished our journey, walking the labyrinth in a garden. The labyrinth was below a three-hundred-year-old mango tree, surrounded by gardens. None of us spoke, all of us still somewhere else, in our visions. On the bus though, returning to the hotel, I sat beside a young woman who might have been about Rae's age, if she were still alive. She had long sandy blonde hair and was thin and tall, like Rae. I introduced myself. "I'm Glen."

She was looking at a tattoo on my arm, of a robot — a replica of a drawing Rae had made before she died. Underneath it is her signature. The young woman looked up at me and said, "That's my middle name. I'm Rae."

At the bottom of the ocean, at depths of twenty thousand feet or more — so far down, so cold, so dark, under such pressure that it's nearly impossible for humans to explore — there are hydrothermal vents, releasing hot water into the depths. Little life thrives in these black, warm places. *Little life.*

But the life that is there includes bacteria that provides the food base for an entire web of life where there is no sunlight and no photosynthesis. These bacteria convert methane into calcium carbonate, taking methane that has seeped out of the earth and into the oceans, and transforming it to a solid form. Methane is among the most potent greenhouse gasses, so these tiny bacteria are doing us all a great favour, nullifying it before it reaches the surface and the atmosphere. I spent most of my life on or near the oceans. I would never have guessed that down there, where we least expect it, in its deepest and darkest depths, there is a world being healed.

In my therapy with Jesse, I chose a new safe place, a home to always return to. I released that boy in the field, who was me all along, trying to be someone I was not. My new safe spot, where I go whenever I can, is near that healing ocean. I am staring up at the stars, feeling the sweet breath of the breeze, and Rae is lying beside me in a lawn chair, telling me about the vastness of the universe, and how little we know.

When she finally stops talking, I whisper to her: "No matter what universe you're in, you are loved. Rae, I'm so glad we chose each other."

— *Glen*

Epilogue

On September 22, 2014, Zachery pleaded guilty of one count of making child pornography. On November 13, 2014, he received a one-year conditional discharge. The court also ordered him to send a letter of apology, which included this passage: "I know no apology I can offer will bring Rehtaeh back. Throughout the course of my life, this will continue to affect me because one moment had such an impact on many people's lives. This makes me realize how valuable life is and it hurts me that I couldn't tell Rehtaeh how sorry I am, or that I couldn't help her afterwards. As youths we sometimes don't realize how fast things can change. This doesn't excuse my actions but I wish you both to know I am sincerely a better man."

On November 24, 2014, Brandon was convicted of one count of distributing child pornography. In January 2015, he received a suspended sentence and one-year probation. He offered no apology, instead claiming he's not responsible for Rehtaeh's death.

The *Independent Review of the Police and Prosecution Response to the Rehtaeh Parsons Case*, written by Murray Segal, was released on October 8, 2015. It found a number of faults in the investigation and made many recommendations for the handling of similar cases.

Notably, Rehtaeh's first police interview didn't follow police protocol. No child protection officer or social worker was present, which for a child under the age of sixteen is mandatory, and the police officer present took only notes, not a recording.

Leah was present, as well, which also didn't follow protocol. As Segal noted, "There can be many other reasons for excluding parents from the child's interview, including: the children may be embarrassed to say certain things in front of a parent or other adult known to them; they may want to appease their parents...while it is impossible for us to know, this error may have very well had an impact in the present case. Rehtaeh's first statement may indeed be unreliable in certain respects, which may explain inconsistencies between that statement and the statement she later provided to the investigator."

One of those inconsistencies was the question of whether Rehtaeh had clearly expressed a lack of consent in the first interview. Segal found that while the second interview was more forceful in that regard, Rehtaeh was clear about the lack of consent in the first as well.

In the summer of 2012, Officer Snair told the family that there was conflicting evidence. That evidence was from Amanda, whose account of the night in question differed from Rehtaeh's. In the judicial review, Segal cautioned police against accepting verbatim accounts of minor-aged witnesses, encouraging them to weigh the testimonies against potential personal agendas that could distort the accuracy of the events in question.

Following the first interview, the decision was made to route Rehtaeh's case to the Sexual Assault Investigation Team of the Halifax Regional Police. At that time, the Internet Crime Unit, which would handle cases of child pornography, was a distinct unit from SAIT. In his report, Segal recommended that these two units work jointly. Officer Snair did not have training in investigating sexual assault claims, only taking these courses after Rehtaeh's case was initially closed. Segal recognized in his report that any officer assigned to a sexual assault unit should have such training and recommended training in technology and cybercrimes involving sexual exploitation as well.

The report further concluded that Rehtaeh should never have been asked to obtain the photograph. Rehtaeh asked another girl to send it to her — a photo of a night she barely remembered. Besides essentially asking her to commit criminal offences herself by asking that girl to send it to her and then being in possession of child pornography, it had the obvious effect of re-traumatizing her. It was one of the most painful moments in her entire ordeal.

In 2016, Glen Canning filed a Freedom of Information request for access to Rehtaeh's RCMP file. The police responded several times, saying they were in the process of releasing the file. It wasn't until the summer of 2019 that Glen received the file, yet almost all of the information had been redacted.

Glen filed several complaints with the police and the Canadian government seeking access to the full and non-redacted police file, so far to no avail. His complaints filed with the Office of the Information Commissioner of Canada were dismissed as unfounded. A police representative told Glen that due to privacy issues, a non-redacted file could not be given to the family for another twenty years.

Rehtaeh's case sparked a number of changes in how law enforcement, health-care providers, and schools deal with allegations of sexual assault and cyberbullying in Canada.

A new course on trauma-informed responses to sexualized violence was offered to police officers in Nova Scotia in 2014. The training stressed that first responders should only gather basic information, so the victim does not have to go through more interviews than required. As Segal writes, "The course, which was intended to bring consistency to HRP [Halifax Regional Police] and RCMP practices, also reinforced that this approach should be used with children."

Cole Harbour District High School had refused to become involved in stopping the circulation of the photograph, since the incident happened off of school grounds and the bullying was online. Nova Scotia's Education Act was later amended, as Segal wrote, "to clarify that schools can intervene when cyberbullying occurs off school grounds if it significantly disrupts the learning climate" — which, in Rehtaeh's case, it certainly did.

Rehtaeh's story also spawned the creation of numerous groups and organizations worldwide focused on raising awareness of teen sexual assault and online exploitation. They include Teens Against Bullying and several branches of the ManUp Campaign, a young men's high school group committed to stopping gender-based violence and fostering positive role models.

Lucy DeCoutere, an actor on the Nova Scotia–filmed television show *Trailer Park Boys*, decided to come forward with allegations of assault against Jian Ghomeshi, saying she was inspired by Rehtaeh's story. Ironically, Ghomeshi was represented by the same firm whose lawyers worked with Murray Segal on Rehtaeh's judicial review.

Glen Canning has gone on to become an international speaker on gender violence, cyberbullying, and cyber exploitation. He has spoken to dozens of schools, universities, conferences, and community groups around the world. He has also participated in police training on sexual violence and cyber exploitation. In 2015, he gave a presentation to the United Nations General Assembly in New York City about gender violence.

Glen's sister, Kim, and his sister-in-law, Shari, went on to launch a charitable organization, Rae of Light Havens, in which families donate their cottages or vacation homes for women and families dealing with domestic violence and sexual assault. These families can stay for free for a week or longer, allowing them an opportunity to heal, be safe, and relax.

Glen and Leah would like to extend their condolences to the family of RCMP Constable Heidi Stevenson, who was murdered in April 2020 in Canada's largest-ever mass killing. She was the officer on the scene at Rehtaeh's first suicide attempt, and later volunteered to assist with the family's memorial walks.

Leah and Glen and their two families are still close. They both honour their daughter's memory by keeping her story alive and committing themselves to making sure what happened to Rehtaeh happens to no other child.

Krista and Glen live in Toronto with their amazing pug, Alice.

Acknowledgements

It would be impossible for me to thank and acknowledge all the people who have offered their support and kindness during the past eight years, the most difficult time in my life.

The outpouring following Rehtaeh's death came from all over the world and I am eternally grateful for it.

This hasn't been an easy story to write, so a very special thank you goes to Susan McClelland for taking a chance with me. Thanks as well to Matt, Alan, Julie, and everyone at Goose Lane for all your hard work in publishing this book.

I'd like to thank former Nova Scotia Member of Parliament Robert Chisholm for leading a moment of silence for Rehtaeh in Canada's Parliament and for supporting our family.

Thanks to Dr. Renée Hložek, astrophysicist at the University of Toronto, for sharing your knowledge about the vastness of our universe.

Deepest thanks to the Avalon Sexual Assault Centre in Halifax for your kindness, care, and ongoing support to those who need help.

I am truly honoured to have a network of friends that has grown to include some of Canada's hardest-working feminists and changemakers. Julie Lalonde, Kevin Vowles, and Farrah Khan. Thank you for making our world better.

Aaron Leach and Travis Wing for inspiring the young men in your life to stand up and be part of something truly important. To know so many young men heard Rehtaeh's story and asked what they can do to change the world healed my heart. To everyone involved with the ManUp program — thank you!

Special thanks to Rehtaeh's friends Jenna, Megan, Breonna, Bryony, Dawid, Susan, Bailee, Emma, and Ashlee. You stood by her when no one else would.

Thank you to Jason Barnes who tried so hard to save Rehtaeh's life on a night that is permanently etched in our minds.

Thank you Anonymous — you heard a cry for help and stood with us as true allies.

My therapist, Jesse Hanson, who shined a light into my soul and helped me find the cracks. I have never felt so whole and it's a blessing I could never repay. Thank you with all my heart!

The support from my loving family has been a constant source of strength. Thank you to my mom, Ivy, and my siblings Steve, Jim, Kim, and Casey.

Jim and Shari, thank you for providing a safe place for me and Krista to share our deepest pain — you helped us to find light again.

Leah, we share a love for Rehtaeh that is as indescribable as it is boundless. As her parents, I am forever grateful that we will always remain connected, not just to Rehtaeh, but also to you and the girls, through that love.

To the seventeen-year-old that received Rehtaeh's heart, thank you for your letter. Go far, enjoy your life to the fullest, and dance as often as you can. Life is beautiful and the world is amazing. Take it all in.

Most of all, I want to thank my wife Krista. Your patience, guidance, and loving heart are the only reason I'm at the place I am today. I hate to think where my path would have taken me if not for your gentle hand on my shoulder to calm me down. You are the light of my life.